PRAISE FOR
Experiencing Friendship with God

"*Experiencing Friendship with God* is an answered prayer for the countless people who have longed to know God in a way that is deeply personal. Faith Eury Cho gives them the *how*. She breaks down, in a beautifully tangible way, how to approach true intimacy with God—a closeness that isn't rooted in fear or servitude, but in friendship. This is truly a powerful guide on how to live and dwell with God, a 'how to abide in God with longevity and peace' book. I'm excited for the thousands of people who will find respite in this book. A must-read for all believers."

—Kobe Campbell, licensed trauma therapist and author of *Why Am I Like This?*

"Faith Eury Cho writes with boldness, and her passion and zeal for the Lord are evident on every page. With practical tools along the way, Cho takes you through the journey of understanding your purpose, discerning God's presence, and living transformed as a close friend of Jesus. You'll be inspired to experience a genuine friendship with God."

—Rebekah Lyons, bestselling author of *Rhythms of Renewal* and *Building a Resilient Life*

"The thing about Faith Eury Cho is that when you read her writing or follow her on social media, you have the immediate feeling that you'd be good friends. And I can confirm that you're not wrong, she is as wise and compassionate as she seems. But I suspect that she's a good friend because she's been friended well by God. And I know from my own experience that friendship with God often deepens where we least expect it: the wilderness. Cho is a kind guide to help us explore the riches of what can be when it comes to our friend and Savior, Jesus. You'll love this book—I've just got a feeling."

—JESS CONNOLLY, author of *You Are The Girl For The Job* and *Breaking Free From Body Shame*

"Too many of us grew up with a false version of God, thinking He is mean and upset with us all the time. Unfortunately, that has robbed our faith in ways that's crushing an entire generation. Thankfully, Faith Eury Cho has reminded us that God's Presence is not only kind but also healing, good, and available to us all. I hope you press into these words long enough to be reminded of who our God really is. I believe it'll redeem and grow your faith."

—TONI COLLIER, speaker, podcast host, and author of *Brave Enough to Be Broken*

"In a Christian culture awash with spiritual self-help books and messages, the church is in dire need of teachers who are determined to take us deeper. Faith Eury Cho is just such a voice. This prolonged meditation on the Presence of God is a tender and refreshing exploration of that which our souls truly crave. If you have ever longed for a better understanding of this essential doctrine, this book is for you. And as her debut book, what an encouragement to us all that Cho is only just getting started!"

—SHARON HODDE MILLER, author of *The Cost of Control*

EXPERIENCING
FRIENDSHIP
WITH GOD

EXPERIENCING FRIENDSHIP WITH GOD

How the Wilderness
Draws Us to His Presence

FAITH EURY CHO

WATERBROOK

A WaterBrook Trade Paperback Original

Published in the United States by WaterBrook, an imprint of Random House, a division of Penguin Random House LLC.

WATERBROOK and colophon are registered trademarks of Penguin Random House LLC.

LIBRARY OF CONGRESS CATALOGING-IN-PUBLICATION DATA
Names: Cho, Faith Eury, author.
Title: Experiencing friendship with God: how the wilderness draws us to His presence / Faith Eury Cho.
Description: First edition. | Colorado Springs: WaterBrook, an imprint of Random House, a division of Penguin Random House LLC, [2023] | Includes bibliographical references.
Identifiers: LCCN 2023009332 | ISBN 9780593445570 (Trade Paperback; acid-free paper) | ISBN 9780593445587 (Ebook)
Subjects: LCSH: God (Christianity)—Worship and love. | God (Christianity)—Knowableness. | Jesus Christ—Presence. | Intimacy (Psychology)—Religious aspects—Christianity. | Suffering—Religious aspects—Christianity.
Classification: LCC BV4817 .C46 2023 | DDC 248.3—dc23/eng/20230512
LC record available at https://lccn.loc.gov/2023009332

Printed in the United States of America on acid-free paper

waterbrookmultnomah.com

2 4 6 8 9 7 5 3 1

Most WaterBrook books are available at special quantity discounts for bulk purchase for premiums, fundraising, and corporate and educational needs by organizations, churches, and businesses. Special books or book excerpts also can be created to fit specific needs. For details, contact specialmarketscms@penguinrandomhouse.com.

To the Holy Spirit, my everything.
You are the reason I live, and these words exist because of You.
Thank You for Your friendship and for loving me to life.

I t was March 2020, and the world had shut down. There was so much fear, confusion, and anxiety about the future, and I was giving my first pandemic all-staff talk in what became affectionately known as the Upper Zoom Room. Scrolling through, I looked at our global team—all 160 people from 19 offices in 15 nations. The team was full of young individuals who had been working tirelessly to abolish slavery everywhere forever. They were some of the most gifted, talented, passionate, committed, and hardworking people I knew. Still, I could hear their concerns:

> *"How can we reach vulnerable people, rescue survivors, and restore the victims of human trafficking if we are in lockdown?"*

"How will traffickers be stopped?"
"What about our funding?"
*"How will we pay for the programs to keep the
    mission moving forward?"*

Our frontline operations ceased overnight. We had goals for the year that now seemed unattainable. Like everyone else on the planet, we had no warning, no control, and no idea what would happen next. But we did still have the only thing we really needed—we had the Presence of God.

I told our team that although everything had changed externally, nothing had changed internally, because we always had been a ministry led by the Presence of God. My husband, Nick, and I were in no way shaken by what was happening because we knew the same God that had led us this far would continue to lead us forward.

I read Zechariah 9:12 to them: "Return to your stronghold, O prisoners of hope; today I declare that I will restore to you double" (ESV). I reminded them that our stronghold is Jesus, because He is our hope, which is an anchor for our soul, and that we had to become prisoners of hope once again. This was an opportunity for everyone to see that God would do what only He could do and that it had always been Him at the helm.

So many of them had joined the mission once we had a large global footprint, not really understanding that it was not marketing, budgeting, planning, staffing, technology, organizational systems, or structures that had brought us to where we were—as good and necessary as those things are. It always was God and always would be Him. We did not need to lose our peace or joy or hope, because even in lockdown, we had the one thing that was the most precious—Jesus.

Nick and I were saved and called long before there was the internet or social media. From the outset, we learned the power of seeking the face of God in a secret place, in order to hear the voice of God and to determine His will and direction for our lives, marriage, family, and ministry. Our ministry has grown, developed, and become more complex, but one thing has never changed, and it is the distinctive that has always guided us— the Presence of God. It is God's Presence that has sustained me through periods of trauma, grief, loss, betrayal, disappointment, failure, warfare, and success.

It is only through intimacy with God that we learn to trust and obey Him, to do what He has called us to do, and to be whom He has called us to be. Those who know their God do great things (Daniel 11:32).

This book contains the most important message this generation needs to hear. Faith Eury Cho is an incredible woman of God and lives and breathes this message. Listen to her and pursue Jesus with everything you have. He will satisfy your deepest needs and longings. He alone is worthy of all honor and glory. He is the goal. He is the prize.

Grace and peace.

CHRISTINE CAINE
Founder of A21 and Propel Women

CONTENTS

CONTENTS

PART 3:
LIVING AS A FRIEND OF GOD

There is no sweeter manner of living in the world than continuous communion with God.

—BROTHER LAWRENCE, *The Practice of the Presence of God*

"What is the point?"

This was my desperate search for meaning in the hospital after I gave birth to my second child. Just hours before, my husband and I had walked into the labor-and-delivery wing, fully confident that all would be well. We had gone through the childbirth routine before, so we were already prepared to celebrate with our newborn son in our arms. Labor came a month earlier than expected, but we had no concerns— just excitement. We were joyfully confident that God was with us, having also the prayers of loved ones who waited in anticipation. There were smiles and laughter in the delivery room.

Yet when my son arrived, trauma crashed the party. The room immediately noticed the concerning shades of purple and blue on his face, so the nurses whisked him away for tests.

I was left to recover in silent confusion. My mind scrambled to process what was happening. Unfortunately, I wasn't able to hold my son until twenty-four hours later, and even then, it wasn't without the tubes, wires, and beeping machines that were required to keep him stable in the intensive care unit. Disappointment clouded my spirit, and I asked, "Why would God allow this?" What was the purpose of this darkness?

I was a firm believer that God can heal, and in my several years as a pastor, I had witnessed and experienced God doing the inexplicable countless times. So, there I was, in my fragile post-delivery state, begging Jesus to do what I knew would be easy for Him.

"Lord, please heal my son."

I thought it was a reasonable ask. Yet not long after this prayer, a nurse walked into the recovery room to deliver more disappointing news. The test results weren't promising, and they needed to increase his oxygen to support his premature lungs. Under the pressure of my dismay, sorrow began mutating into frustration. Where was God? Was my plea not heard? Did my years of serving the church not merit this one favor?

I continued to plead, "Lord, please heal my son."

What was supposed to be a celebration with friends and family in the hospital turned into days of weeping in a dark room with my cellphone endlessly buzzing with sad-face emojis and well wishes. Each day, doctors and nurses came in to explain why more blood work needed to be done and why taking him home wasn't an option. Their matter-of-fact explanations were void of compassion, just as the room felt like it was void of God. Eventually, my desperate prayers slowed to a resentful silence. I had called, but He refused to answer—or so it felt. Perhaps my screaming silence would be heard instead.

At this point in my life, I had been a preacher of the good

news for years, but I discovered how a moment that strikes just the right nerve can unveil the fragility of one's trust in God. Grief took away every religious propriety I had and reduced me to an angry mother holding a grudge against God in her hospital bed. Although I was an experienced Bible teacher, my understanding of His Presence wasn't robust enough to keep my hope breathing in this hour. Even when friends came by to surround my husband and me with fervent intercession, I merely stared at the foot of the bed as my hot tears flowed in protest. What makes sense in the pews doesn't always seem to add up when you are facing the ugly realities of life. I was ready to forfeit. The sorrow was so deep and the fear was so demanding that I could only conclude that God had abandoned me. It didn't feel as if He was there, and even if He was, it wasn't enough for me. What if faith bears no visible results during times of despair? What, then, is the point of faith?

Questions like these demand answers because it is a weary soul who asks them, a soul who aches for what is true and real. Anyone asking these questions is increasingly intolerant of religious fluff and niceties, no longer willing to settle for inspirational words but rather aching for authentic change. You don't want a catchy sermon quote when you are dealing with tragedy. You need supernatural help when you are wrestling with anxiety. After you have endured repeated letdowns, one after the other, positive thinking and good strategy feel desperately futile—like holding an umbrella in the face of a tsunami. When you are in this rut in your faith journey, you swiftly swipe away the inspirational social media content on your phone because it doesn't encourage you anymore. You may have attempted to change your attitude, listened to motivational podcasts, and even gone to that conference that promised to take you to new levels, but your life still feels like an endless cycle of the same issues and habits. When your heart is bleeding and your back is bent under a heavy burden, words are just not enough. You need more.

One day turned to three very quickly, and I was told that I wouldn't be able to take my baby boy home from the hospital, that I would have to leave him in the care of nurses and machines while I drove away. My heart could hardly bear it. I needed to storm into the throne room of God. I had a bone to pick with the King. Yet this pent-up angst was dressed in a hospital gown and still vulnerably healing, so I did the only thing I could do—opened my journal and held my pen, although I had no words to write. I had nothing to say, no song to sing. Still, I felt a voice say to me, "Give thanks."

Even though I am a pastor and this was supposed to be my moment to demonstrate great faith in hard times, I am ashamed to say I scoffed at the idea. Being a good example of Christian faith was basically my career, but I had nothing good to say that night. Give thanks for what? My newborn child was going through a mysterious health crisis and needed a machine to breathe! I couldn't stand the injustice of it all.

I felt the voice again. "Give thanks."

So, I reluctantly mustered up the strength to write an obligatory list.

Thank You for the nurses.
Thank You for the clean hospital room.
Thank You for lunch. It was sushi—my favorite.

Eventually, this obligatory list became more elaborative as I paused to appreciate the friends and family who were contending for us in prayer.

Thank You for the kindness of those who are praying
    for us right now.
Thank You for this time spent with my husband. It
    has been meaningful, and we've grown much
    closer.

What started off as half-hearted list-making turned into an immersive meditation on all the good that was for me and with me. My list of thanksgiving that I thought was for Jesus was actually His love letter to me. Forty more minutes of writing passed, and my heart thawed. It was as if wind began filling the sails of a ship becalmed on glassy water. An unraveling began as I started to recognize the signs of God's steadfast care all over my life. Oh, how He loved me! How kind He had been all this time! I became profoundly aware that, right there in that hospital room, I was before the blazing, shining Presence of Jesus. I used to think that choosing to be grateful in the midst of hardship was just choosing to be blind to one's problems. In this moment, however, I realized that it is choosing to recognize God's fingerprints on our lives.

That night, not only did I know that He was with me, but I also felt it. It felt like a firm, warm hug, the kind that makes you feel safe and seen. During my journaling, another nurse walked in to tell me that my son wasn't doing any better. Regardless, I kept scribbling the evidence that proved God was still with me because my heart was immersed in love.

It was enough.

My purpose in that moment was to know Him—not in theory but in friendship. Jesus is the point. He is the reward. Knowing His Presence is the purpose of the wilderness. This revelation was God's gift to me in that dark hospital room. Another gift came a week later when I was able to take my healthy, growing boy out of the NICU and to his own crib at home.

The Wilderness

This hospital experience with my son later allowed me to resonate with the pain of those who walk out of churches or change religions and shut the door on Jesus. Truth is, from now until heaven, the harsh realities of life will constantly challenge our belief in Him. You will fail, and sometimes other people will fail you. Plans will fall through. Doors will close with no indication of opening again. Circumstances won't budge in your favor, and certain people may never change. You may be in a waiting season or, perhaps, a crushing season. If this remains your reality long enough, then you arrive at the same juncture that I came to while my child was on a breathing machine— disillusioned with a burned-out faith. This is the wilderness of the soul.

For the Israelites, the wilderness was an eleven-day trip that took forty years.* The Hebrew people abandoned the rule of Pharaoh in Egypt to trust the rule of Yahweh, their God, hoping for a better lot in life. The miracles of God and the leadership of Moses interrupted years of oppression, and the Israelites left all they had ever known to cross the Red Sea to freedom. However, this wasn't a convenient, predictable journey that quickly led them to greener pastures. Instead, they followed Yahweh into the unknown, although at that time the uncertainty was eclipsed by the bright hope of the Promised Land ahead, "a land flowing with milk and honey."†

The wilderness is a familiar scene in the Bible, for it was a

---

* Deuteronomy 1:2.
† Exodus 3:8.

place where many of God's servants reached the end of themselves and encountered God. Hagar cried there while she helplessly waited to lose her son to thirst.* Elijah prayed for death there while fear exhausted him.† The Israelites' wilderness journey wasn't a hike along a scenic trail with a sunset that you could capture for Instagram. It wasn't a place of respite with lovely views and adventure. No, for the Hebrews in the Mediterranean Middle East, the wilderness was a horrific wasteland that offered little chance for survival. It was an inhospitable region with bullying heat and desolate terrain. It would be hard to nurture a dream there and even harder to find a purpose.

The wilderness of the soul is no different. When in it, you travel across the wasteland of discouragement. Very few, if any, will fully understand your journey, which is why loneliness becomes an unwelcome friend there. You become familiar with pain rather than progress, confusion rather than vision. Some say pain makes you stronger, but this is a senseless platitude for someone who is sapped of strength while wandering. You might be naturally sure of yourself, but in the wilderness, you are met with destabilizing uncertainty. To make it worse, you aren't sure when it will end.

After reading about the rest of the Israelites' wilderness wandering in the Old Testament, you would know that many travelers, including Moses, never made it to the Promised Land. Consequently, you could consider this journey pointless because it wasn't a victory march toward the blessed end. Instead, it was a drawn-out journey filled with twists and turns—and much fear and failure.

So, what was the wilderness for? What was the point?

The wilderness exposed Israel's rebellious pride and disobe-

* Genesis 21:14–19.
† 1 Kings 19:1–9.

dience, but if that was the point of it all, then they followed God out of slavery only to die in shame. Furthermore, if the wilderness was just the means to get to a better place, then it was an inefficient journey, one that must have felt like forty years of purgatory until God finally considered them worthy of the reward. The sojourning would have been a waste for an entire generation who believed the hopelessness of the wilderness more than the promises of God, then died in unbelief before they could set foot on the promise fulfilled. If this were the actual purpose of our difficult seasons—either to be destroyed by our own depravity or to earn our way into greener pastures—then remaining in slavery might be the better option.

Beloved wanderer, what if the ultimate purpose of the wilderness isn't just to be better or to get somewhere? Although hardship can prepare us for the fulfillment of His promises, the only reason the wilderness ultimately makes sense is the same reason Christianity makes sense. Israel didn't leave Egypt just to arrive at a desired destination and wait for eternity stably and happily. And although sanctification is indeed a by-product of walking through a desert season, the pain of the journey isn't merely the cruel means to that end. Rather, the purpose of the wilderness is to know the Presence of God, and an intimate, authentic, and passionate friendship with Him is the reward.

A French Monk and an Asian American Girl

Admittedly, at one point in my life, if someone had told me that to befriend Jesus was the ultimate reward of my faith, I would have been underwhelmed. Because I am writing on the Presence of God, you may think that it came naturally to me or that I have always been on some heavenly cloud nine with Jesus. False. I was the one who would watch church members cry as they worshipped while I wondered why God wasn't having the same effect on me. I didn't always know how to enjoy prayer, and I thought He directly spoke only with special, spiritual people.

I wanted this to change, but it seemed that every sermon or book I turned to ended with some rendition of "Pray a lot" or "Just go to Jesus." What I really needed was someone to usher me into His Presence and help me navigate the mysteries of getting to know Him personally. A pivotal part of my spiritual journey was when I ran into a book called *The Practice of the Presence of God* by Brother Lawrence of the Resurrection. I found it in a bookstore, and it was small—really, really small. Honestly, I bought it because of that very reason. A few minutes into the book, I realized it was written by a monk who enjoyed a deep friendship with Jesus. His pleasure and excitement jumped through the pages. I wanted what he had. Brother Lawrence seemed to have reached the Mount Everest of spirituality, yet his maxims were profoundly simple—almost childlike. They were simple truths applied to the simple life of a Carmelite monk from the seventeenth century. I didn't know it then, but the Lord had commissioned me into my own lifelong journey of befriending His Presence in today's increasingly complicated times. This book is the fruit of that journey so far. I hope it helps you fulfill your life's purpose. Although you can aspire to easier and better days, your purpose isn't found there. No matter what terrain of life you tread, your reason for existence is to access the gift of the gospel, which is to know His Presence—intimately, authentically, and passionately. This gift is yours to access today; it is also yours to access in the wilderness. It wasn't just for a monk living in the seventeenth century; it was also for a millennial Asian American girl living in the twenty-first century. *And it is also for you.*

PART 1

The Purpose of the Wilderness

CHAPTER 1

Created for His Presence

> All that I sought, all this world relentlessly pursues in all
> the wrong places, is found in the presence of God.
>
> —J. Ryan Lister, *The Presence of God*

"The Presence" or "the Presence of God" frequently comes up in Christian jargon and church-speak, but we often miss its meaning. When sung during worship, it can inadvertently sound as if He is an energy force that we must woo to accrue. When we misbehave or forget Him for an elongated period, it can feel as though He is a commodity that we must rush to regain. Throughout Scripture, the Presence of God has so many names and forms. Is He a burning bush like the one that appeared to Moses?* Is His Presence like the cloud that led Israel through the wilderness?† Is He a gentle whisper like Elijah heard from a cave?‡ The matter of His omnipresence further

* Exodus 3:4.
† Exodus 14:19.
‡ 1 Kings 19:12.

complicates the search. If God is everywhere, are we not always in His Presence? To seek Him, then, sounds as redundant and unnecessary as seeking air. However, to Brother Lawrence, our dear Carmelite lay brother, the Presence of God was a friend to know intimately, and doing so was "the life and nourishment of the soul."*

Indeed, God is everywhere, in the galaxies above and the waves below. As time and space exist, so does God. But this boundless Creator also desires to be present with His people. The Presence of God can be encountered and known by humankind. The God who is holy and infinite chooses to be relationally accessible to His creation. He is entitled to remain aloof from all that is beneath Him, and He could do so because He is fully self-sufficient. However, from Genesis to Revelation, we see a God who is constantly speaking, helping, comforting, defending, and providing. He is God, but He chose to be Emmanuel—God with us.

When we refer to the Presence of God, we aren't speaking of an emotionally charged moment or "a vibe." It isn't a religious achievement reserved for monks, nor is it a feel-good saying that you sprinkle onto your church traditions. The Presence of God is God Himself, including His character, emotions, and thoughts. The Presence used to dwell with His people through the means of a covenant arrangement, with priests as intermediaries and amid the shadows of a tabernacle. Later, He became the God who dwelled among His people in a temple. Eventually, He came as a man named Jesus. And today those who say yes to Jesus also say yes to an everlasting friendship with the Holy Spirit, who remains with them through thick and thin.

* Brother Lawrence, *The Practice of the Presence of God* (New Kensington, Pa.: Whitaker House, 1982), 67.

When we choose to follow Jesus, we are offered the gift of experiencing the treasures of the gospel. Just as beavers are designed to build and birds are meant to fly, we are created to know our Creator—intimately, authentically, and passionately. Communing with Him breathes life into our bones. To know Him is to know peace. He is the wisdom above all logic. He is the pleasure above all earthly satisfaction. He is the love that makes our lives make sense. Thanks to what Jesus has done, this gift is accessible to us who accept Him as Lord and Savior.

I have sat for hours with a dear friend who has always celebrated my God-victories and cheered me on in everything I do for the church. I love and respect her deeply. Yet when it comes to knowing Jesus for herself, she always kindly declines. She doesn't like the thought of devoting her life to Christ, and she prefers to connect with her idea of the Divine through nature, rituals, meditation, etc. Seeking truth through her own means feels more freeing than submitting to the Truth. She looks for signs in order to feel close to God. Yet that desire to be linked to the Endless and Eternal doesn't come from within but rather is given to us by our Creator. This is why the gospel is such good news. God desires to connect with us intentionally and personally. What Jesus accomplished on the cross provided a doorway for you to have direct access to Him, to hear His words and know Him for yourself. His Presence is His intentional dwelling with us. As humans, we were never meant to look to the universe for signs and to hope for its random mercies. That isn't what we were created for. God doesn't offer us shadows of the real thing. He offers us Himself.

You were created to know God. This isn't merely cerebral knowledge such as acquiring fancy theological concepts and biblical information. It also isn't superficial knowledge like knowing a celebrity or a politician from afar. Rather, knowing the Presence of God is an intimate connection that isn't of this world. It isn't magical, but it is indeed mystical. To know God is to know what He means before you exchange a word. To know Him is to see Him with your heart. It isn't the kind of knowing that is shared by colleagues or neighbors. To know Jesus is to experience a deep and consistent closeness. Nothing can fulfill you more. This is God's intentional design for your being. To recognize this design and prioritize your life accordingly allows you to enjoy the fruit of faith no matter how desolate the wilderness you face.

Your very existence is meant to be fueled by a friendship with God. This friendship can give your spirit more energy than the freshest cup of coffee. It can be where you find the inspiration to create, the direction to make decisions, and the wisdom to build a life on this earth. To experience Him should be to know beauty. To hear from Him should be your soul's food. To obey Him should be a sustaining joy. He is infinite, so to know Him is an endless unveiling of riches. A relationship with Him can charge your every inhale and exhale. This is how we were created. This is how it was meant to be. This should be our only fuel, but that all too often isn't the case. Let's explore what fuels us.

Recognizing the Wrong Fuel

I once accidentally put diesel in my car. Yep, you got that right. I put the sort of fuel that belongs in semitrucks and boats into my brand-new little Honda Accord coupe. I was a sixteen-year-old first-time driver who had no clue there was even a difference between gasoline and diesel. All I knew was that the button was red and it was cheaper (at that time)! It seemed like a no-brainer until I started to drive out of the gas station. It took about a minute for my car to slow down and emit some suspicious clicking sounds. Meanwhile, I kept pumping the accelerator, my way of denying what was going on and trying to push through. It should come as no surprise that I failed to push through. Thankfully, I was able to roll my way into a parking lot before my car came to a dead stop. It wasn't long before the mechanic gathered the data and figured out that my car was running on the wrong fuel.

I had put the wrong fuel in my car without realizing it, and you may be doing the same with your life. Any motivation or purpose that isn't centered on knowing His Presence is like diesel to a Honda Accord. Counterfeits or watered-down versions of the real thing are easy to reach, and it may even seem fine while you are filling up. However, these motivations will eventually fail us. For your life to run optimally and according to its God-given design, your friendship with God must be your highest priority and the center of all that you do.

Taking an honest inventory of your motivations will reveal the fuel that is running your life. This requires a bit of close inspection because some motivations aren't immediately visible and many are reasonable from a worldly perspective. Consider the things that influence your choices. What priorities, hopes, and desires get you through the day? Could they be any of the following?

- your ambition for a stable and blessed life
- your obligation to take care of your family
- your need to belong to someone or to a group of people
- your aspiration to be seen and acknowledged
- your desire to accomplish something worthwhile
- your longing to be worthy

Motivations that aren't centered on His Presence can also be uncovered by looking at our fears. An all-consuming fear of failure can reveal a desperation to achieve. Anxieties over changes and transitions can reveal the need for control. A fear of abandonment might reveal our compulsive need to be accepted and committed to. Fears fool us into believing it is wise to live for anything other than a friendship with His Presence.

Our church and faith lives aren't necessarily free of counterfeit fuels. But counterfeit fuels are the hardest to recognize in these spheres because some motivations are noble and righteous. Attending church, volunteering, and doing the right things are usually inspired by decent intentions, whether to be a helpful member of the community or to be a good person. These are virtuous goals to have, and they aren't a problem in and of themselves. The problem arises when we spend years in the church feeling as if we are abiding in the Lord simply because we are driven by such virtuous goals. As a result, we unknowingly trade a friendship with Jesus for sanctification and service.

Good works, noble character, and wisdom are meant to be the result of our intimacy with His Presence. They aren't the way to achieve that intimacy. Before living to be good or to do good, we must live to know Him. Changing for the better, accruing more Christian knowledge, or giving back to the community are all biblical desires. Yet these, too, cannot be our fuel. Unless we pursue a genuine friendship with God first, trying to do these things doesn't give us life, and at some point, we will find ourselves like my unfortunate Honda Accord coupe. We will burn out. This is because our Creator didn't design us to function this way.

A History of Humanity's Friendship with God

We were built to function from a friendship with God. At the start of their existence, Adam and Eve received an assignment from Him: "Be fruitful and increase in number; fill the earth and subdue it. Rule over the fish in the sea and the birds in the sky and over every living creature that moves on the ground."* This was no small task for those who only recently started breathing! And yet, from the very beginning, humankind was endowed with a calling to be fruitful, increase, subdue, and rule. Talk about ambition and a plan! God had big hopes and dreams for Adam and Eve. He has always been a big-picture sort, a visionary. With a calling like that, the most sensible thing would be to roll up your sleeves and get right to work. However, as we know, that wasn't the way it transpired.

The day after God gave them the commission, they rested.† This is seemingly the opposite of what humankind was meant to do. Where was the forward momentum? Where was the productivity? Instead, their first step toward destiny was spending a day doing nothing productive. It was a holy day, set apart for humankind to be aligned with God. Despite appearances, this didn't contradict their calling nor divert them from their mission. Although it may look like a pause in Adam and Eve's pursuit of their purpose, it was the very fulfillment of that purpose.

We were created to know Him personally and intimately, and our God-given calling is meant to overflow from this very purpose. Adam and Eve had such direct access to God that seeing Him walk through the garden in the cool of the day was no

* Genesis 1:28.
† Genesis 2:2.

strange thing.* That access was the well from which Adam and Eve drew their inspiration and strength to expand the garden and grow in dominion. When they needed a plan, God guided and instructed. When they needed the means to carry out their plan, God provided it. Their commission was enabled by one thing—a friendship with God. They didn't strain for survival, nor did they strive for progress. Everything was the fruit of knowing His heart, daily hearing His voice, and heeding His counsel.

Technically, every creature was in close proximity to God in that garden, for He walked among them too. But God created Adam and Eve to be His friends, which gave them authority over the garden and made it possible for them to be fruitful in it. No other living creature had the agency to discover His will and collaborate with Him each day. Adam and Eve weren't like other created beings; they had the choice to ignore or acknowledge God, just as we do today. When humankind communed with their Maker, a garden grew and spread. Unfortunately, Adam and Eve broke the perfect communion they had with the Father, and ever since, we have been living in a fallen world where humans are still trying to expand their gardens—but without the Presence of God.

Thankfully, our destiny is still to do great things in friendship with God. What is thrilling about the Father's ingenious way of loving us and restoring all things is that, thousands of years after the garden, Jesus gave another commission to His friends:

> All authority in heaven and on earth has been given to me. Therefore go and make disciples of all nations, baptizing them in the name of the Father and of the

* Genesis 3:8.

Son and of the Holy Spirit, and teaching them to obey everything I have commanded you. And surely I am with you always, to the very end of the age.*

Here is another call to God's children to be fruitful, another commission to spread His love and glory over the earth. It is essentially a chance to expand the garden once again but, this time, with a connection to Him that can't be broken by our weaknesses and failures. Here is another commission to expand His kingdom and increase. And again He offers us the only guarantee that matters. He will be with us. He offers His Presence.

The Power of Spiritual Longing

I wasn't born into a Christian home. Having immigrated to America from South Korea at a young age, I was navigating a new world with a new language as a six-year-old in Los Angeles. Every night while I lay in bed, a curious longing brewed in my heart. Each evening as I felt the silence of my room, I would think, *God, are You out there?*

If You're there, can You show up to me right now? I promise I won't tell anyone.

Can You help me understand what my teacher says tomorrow?

Can You hear me?

Where do You live?

What do You look like?

I had never heard a sermon or attended a church service in my life. However, in my heart, there was a longing to know a higher being. I figured that if a deity truly existed, I should be on His good side. I wanted to be His friend, but I didn't know

* Matthew 28:18–20.

how. I didn't know back then what I know now—that the spiritual hunger to know Him is a gift. You may not consider it a gift, because sometimes that longing feels like a void. If you have attempted to fill that void with all sorts of things to no avail, then you may know disappointment quite well. But that void is a good thing. The soul's ache to hear a melody above the cadence of this life is a gift because it means that there is room for Him in your heart. And when you open your heart to Him, He will fill it—always. James 4:8 says, "Come near to God and he will come near to you." And come near He did.

God began revealing Himself to this asker of endless nighttime questions. On a family vacation, I sat on the hotel bed while my parents were packing up our bags. I just happened to be watching a gospel film on cable television, and I asked my mother, "Who is that man on the screen?" She said, "That's Jesus." I said, "He looks like a very nice man." I learned God's name that day. After the trip, I went to the library and asked the librarian if she had any books on Jesus. Oh, the look on the dear old librarian's face at the sight of this little Korean girl asking in broken English how to find books on Jesus. She paused and kindly replied, "Child, you have to go to church to learn about Jesus." So naturally, I began asking my mother to drop me off at church on Sundays.

We are all built with spiritual longing, a desire to be connected to the Divine. It is proof of our God-given design. At every time in human history, there has been some form of spiritual ritual or worship. From the start, humankind has always been reaching for what is beyond the stars. It is in our DNA to seek connection with a being that is greater than we are. No one can claim they aren't spiritual enough to know His Presence. You are built to know Jesus just as you are built to breathe air.

Jesus doesn't neglect spiritual longing, and this book is

proof, for it was written by that little girl who started her faith journey not knowing one Christian or having any biblical knowledge. I didn't know the proper way to worship or pray, but I knew how to want God. That was enough. We have spiritual longing so that He can fulfill it. Step by step, He led me to the right places at the right times so that I could chip away at the mystery that is God. I first discovered His name, and later, I discovered His love—through His provision of the right people, places, and moments.

Spiritual longing can be discouraging if you have no hope that it can lead to more of God. The desire to be more connected to Him can feel like loneliness or emptiness because nothing on earth can quench it. To recognize spiritual longing is also to recognize that life isn't satisfying you, that you want more. It is, at times, uncomfortable, which is why we are quick to dismiss it as a distraction or bury it as if it is an emotional crisis. However, befriending the Presence of God must begin with accepting spiritual longing and listening to its cries. Your soul's pining is an invitation for you to grow in deeper knowledge of your Creator. Even if you were baptized as a child and attend church regularly, your spiritual longing is proof that God has more for you. If you have even a droplet of desire to know Him better, start there. Keep that and stir it. That simple desire is potent with transformative power. You were created to intimately know Jesus, and your very being is aching to be fueled properly.

Show Me Your Glory

Moses knew he couldn't live without the Presence of God. In Exodus 33:15, he said, "If your Presence does not go with us, do not send us up from here." This was the cry of Moses in the wilderness. God had offered him a way out of this arduous journey, but Moses refused to take it. God promised a land flowing with milk and honey to the Israelites, and it was an age-old oath given to Abraham, Isaac, and Jacob. God even offered to send an angel to drive out the enemies that inhabited the land. Israel just had to get up and go.[*]

Exodus 33:3 says, "Go up to the land flowing with milk and honey. But I will not go with you, because you are a stiff-necked people and I might destroy you on the way."

However, this didn't please Moses, because God Himself wouldn't go with them. Moses wouldn't have it. He could have gotten everything a person would want out of life. His people would have been stable, well fed, and fruitful. He would have had a successful political career, and his name would have been renowned for generations. Everything God had promised as they left Egypt was right at his fingertips. God even offered to make this happen supernaturally. But it still wasn't enough for Moses. He said, "Do not send us up from here."

Moses knew that the Promised Land was nothing without the Promise Keeper. He was able to discern this because he knew God better than anyone else did. He met Yahweh in the mystery of the burning bush.[†] He witnessed God's power in the ten plagues against Egypt that set Israel free from slavery.[‡] He saw God's faithfulness in the parting of the Red Sea.[§] Nevertheless, Moses didn't relate to God simply as a miracle-working deliverer of the Hebrew people. His relationship with God wasn't based on the manna that fed them daily or the water that came from a rock to quench their thirst. To Moses, God wasn't just a solution to a problem. Instead, God was his friend.

* Exodus 33:1–3.
† Exodus 3.
‡ Exodus 7–11.
§ Exodus 14:21–31.

Whenever Moses had to meet Him, he would go into the tent of meeting and they would speak "face to face, as one speaks to a friend."* Moses knew the Presence of God, personally and authentically, and this was enough for him to know that the Promised Land without Yahweh was meaningless. Moses knew that Israel's greatest good wasn't provision or stability; neither was it to be known as a powerful nation that could conquer all their enemies. Simply put, there was no Israel without God, because God was the point of Israel's existence. Just as Adam and Eve's purpose was to be with their Creator, Israel's purpose was to be with Yahweh.

It is possible to find ourselves choosing the Promised Land over the Presence, the blessings that come with God rather than God Himself. In fact, would it be unreasonable to think that sometimes we draw near to our Father only because we want to get to the Promised Land? Perhaps sober introspection would reveal that we are attending church for the answered prayers and praising Jesus to earn some help through tough times. Although these blessings undoubtedly come with who God is, they do so by grace, not by a transaction of faithfulness. The goal of our devotion to Christ must be nothing other than friendship and intimacy with Him. At the end of the day, if your faith gave you only Jesus, would that be enough?

Church was always meant to be a gathering of people who seek His Presence and live His ways. Yet too often it isn't that. If the Presence of God isn't the purpose of the gathering, then the church has become a wishing well for our needs and wants. The ultimate reward for our existence isn't the life that we build here. Rather, it is the One who isn't of this world. It is time to check what we really believe about His Presence today. It is time to check our fuel.

* Exodus 33:11.

Already Blessed

The wilderness of the soul is a far cry from a pleasant experience. Yet there is some good news if you are wandering through a wasteland. Numbers 6:22–27 says,

> The LORD said to Moses, "Tell Aaron and his sons, 'This is how you are to bless the Israelites. Say to them:
>
> "'"The LORD bless you
>   and keep you;
> the LORD make his face shine on you
>   and be gracious to you;
> the LORD turn his face toward you
>   and give you peace."'
>
> "So they will put my name on the Israelites, and I will bless them."

This was the blessing God had for His people from the start of their trek. After Israel left Egypt, they temporarily stayed at Sinai, where God gave marching orders to Moses. Those instructions included this priestly blessing that Aaron and his sons were to give to the people. Throughout their wandering, as the Israelites set up camp, broke camp, and bore children without a permanent home to settle in, this was the blessing they received on a regular basis. There is no mention of a land flowing with milk and honey. Instead, it is about the reward of knowing God.

When I was on the high school swim team, we would oftentimes stand at each end of the pool to cheer on our teammates in the race. Especially for the long-distance races, we would shout encouragement such as "Almost there!" or "Get it!" implying that the racers were still on the way. Once the races were over, our encouragement would turn to celebration because the swimmers made it to the end and there wasn't a lap left to strive for. The blessing that we see in Numbers 6 is the equivalent of saying "You made it!" because Israel already had the treasure. As they were wandering and waiting for the land flowing with milk and honey, they weren't waiting to be blessed. Israel was *already* blessed.

This is good news. This means that we, too, are blessed now, before the breakthroughs happen and the upgrades arrive. We can experience the pleasures of His Presence today, before any of the problems get fixed or the worrying situations go away. Your blessing isn't lost in the past, nor are you working for it to arrive in the future. You no longer must wait and hope to be blessed. You have the blessing, thanks to Jesus. Just as Moses had access to the Presence of God, you have access to the Holy Spirit by grace through faith. Your pilgrimage is not to attain something you don't have but rather to grow in awareness of and intimacy with it forever.

Beloved, are you experiencing His Presence daily? Do you know the incredible release from shame when you encounter the kindness of His forgiveness? Do you know His loyalty to you in the face of your character flaws and misjudgments? Do you know the gentleness in His voice when He speaks life into your weary soul? Do you know the intricate genius of His wisdom when you are at a loss for what to do? How about the comfort of the Holy Spirit as you grieve loss?

Let's check our fuel today. You may know many things about God but fall short in knowing Him on a personal level. The world's currents are always going to pull you away from living out this purpose of experiencing friendship with God.

We are so easily deceived by the significance we get from the things we do and the people we are with. Days that are filled with temporary and secondary matters will leave us continuously running on empty. Busy—but empty.

If you have been away from God or you have known church traditions and spiritual leaders more than you have known your Savior, today is a wonderful day to start your journey back to His Presence. While the process isn't always easy, here are three simple and practical encouragements to help you along the way.

1. Check Your Fuel Honestly

We need to take an honest look at why we do things. Kick-start an inquiry into your whys. Keep unraveling the layers of your motives until you get to your core purpose. Your inquiry might look something like this:

Example 1: *Why do I work hard? → Why does it matter what other people think of me? → Why is my identity so tied to other people's opinions?*

Example 2: *Why do I go to church every week? → Why do I pray more at church than I do at home? → Why do I pray?*

Example 3: *Why do I spend money the way I do? → Why do I feel like money can buy satisfaction?*

If your core purpose isn't a more intimate friendship with God, then there are counterfeit fuels to recognize and remove. Examining our motives is necessary work. We don't want to end up living as strangers to God without being aware of it.

2. Be Intentional

Just like any other relationship, ours with God requires intentionality. What are some things you can do to encourage this desire to develop a deeper friendship with Jesus? Think of things that will naturally fit into your lifestyle. For example, if you set an alarm to pray at the same time each day but you aren't usually around your phone at that time, that wouldn't be the most effective action to take. When it doesn't feel natural to you and your lifestyle, it will be extremely difficult to maintain and add undue pressure. Here are a few ideas on how to be intentional with God:

- If you wouldn't consistently carry around a physical journal, start journaling your prayers on your phone, like personal letters to God.
- If you are a young parent who rarely has a quiet moment to read Scripture, try listening to Scripture while you are watching your children or doing chores.
- If you aren't a morning person, try investing in your friendship with Jesus during the evenings.

3. Avoid Substitutes for God

Be careful not to treat the things of God as a substitute for God. We can spend hours at church, have Christian friends, and consume Christian resources while still never interacting with Him. Listening to a sermon can be a form of hearing from

God, but it can never replace listening to God Himself. The Bible in our hands and on our electronic devices is an open invitation to delve into His words ourselves. The gift of the gospel is that we can access Him personally, not just through others. Reading a book about God is helpful to guide us to Him, but it can't take the place of praying to Him directly. Learning about ourselves can aid the sanctification process as we walk into spiritual maturity, but it can never outweigh the value of knowing Him personally. It is all too easy to feel as if listening to a Christian podcast counts as communing with the Holy Spirit for the day. Listening to other people's thoughts is nice, but it can never replace connecting with Him through our own praise and worship. Let's not trade God for the things of God.

Dear Friend of God

As someone who used to struggle to grasp the purpose of life, I have found that there is nothing more fulfilling than befriending Jesus. However, even as Christians, we can easily miss this. I have found myself in burnout and disillusionment time and time again, and it always came down to this—I was living for a purpose other than knowing my loyal Savior.

Once I aligned myself with this holy agenda of befriending Him, life became more than bearable. There was sweetness even in the mundane, and there was strength in times of pain. I was a young, energetic female preacher full of dreams, so motherhood hit me hard. I didn't realize it at the time, but I had been fueled by ambition. Accomplishments excited me. Getting things done for the kingdom was what got me going. Traveling around the world gave me reason to live. However, when much of that came to a halt, the way I responded to my newfound limitations made me realize that I had been running on counterfeit fuels. I would rock my children at 3 A.M., wondering what the point of life really was. So, I began talking to Jesus. Even though they didn't feel like it at the time, those nights were a gift to me. I spent the most time with the Holy Spirit during those hours—grieving, pondering, sharing, requesting. From the world's perspective, I was unseen and unproductive. But from heaven's perspective, I was fulfilling my very purpose because I was communing with Him. It was a gritty and messy season of discovering all my counterfeit fuels and going back to living for a friendship with Jesus—the way He created me to live.

You could be going through your difficult season in the hope that self-growth or better days are waiting for you on the other side. These are common aspirations, and it is natural to be driven by these things. However, Christ offers us a better hope. He designed you to be fueled by a friendship with Him. Any dissatisfaction or disillusionment that you may experience in this world is testament to a spiritual longing that can be quenched only by knowing Him—intimately, authentically, and passionately. Living for His Presence was possible for Brother Lawrence in a monastery as well as a very tired mother in a nursery. It is possible for you too.

CHAPTER 2

The Mystery of His Presence

The soul—accustomed by this exercise to the practice of faith—can actually see and feel God by simply entering His presence.

—BROTHER LAWRENCE, *The Practice of the Presence of God*

One night around 1 A.M., I was doing my usual rounds around the home to make sure all the doors were locked and the lights were turned off before I headed to bed. As I was finishing up, I heard a strange noise while going down the hallway—a whimpering. I peeked into my eldest daughter's room to find her sitting on her bed, tearfully mumbling. Alarmed, I rushed to her side to ask what the matter was, to which she replied, "He's stuck!" You can imagine my bewilderment in this moment. So, I asked, "Who's stuck?"

"Jesus. He's stuck!"

"What do you mean?"

"At church, they said that Jesus lives inside of me. But He can't seem to come out so that I can see Him and talk to Him!"

She was around six years old at that time, and it was her first time grappling with the mysteries of His Presence. Everyday sayings like "He lives within you" can feel good when you hear them but can be confusing in practice. Being a Christ-follower isn't an extracurricular activity—it demands the entirety of our lives. Our aspirations, habits, mindsets, and relationships are just a few of the things we must submit to the way of Jesus. However, to live for someone that we know cerebrally but not experientially can be a challenge. As my six-year-old wrestled with her Sunday school theology while praying in the night, she, too, was experiencing the tension of living for a God she doesn't fully understand.

Children aren't the only ones who wrestle with this. How do we befriend the Presence of God? If only it were as simple as seeing His face and hearing His voice directly and clearly. Instead, it requires faith. It is sensing without seeing and hearing without the use of our physical ears. The reality of our faith journey with God is that it is filled with mystery. We are meant to know Him with our spirits, not just with our minds. This kind of knowing can't be imparted to us through a textbook or a sermon.

A. W. Tozer once wrote, "It is simply not enough to know *about* God. We must know God in increasing levels of intimacy that lift us above all reason and into adoration and praise and worship."* To know *about* God is to know doctrines that describe Him. To know Him—intimately, authentically, and passionately—we need more than intellect. To dance with mystery, we need a childlike trust.

---

* A. W. Tozer, *Delighting in God,* ed. James L. Snyder (Bloomington, Minn.: Bethany House, 2015), 17.

The Frustrations in Knowing God

I have penned a myriad of tearful confessions in my journal over the years. In those entries, I would acknowledge a Presence that was with me but in a way that I couldn't fully grasp. During times of heartbreak, I wished He would embrace me. In my moments of failure, I wished it were easy to hear the mercy in His voice. I would have loved to be able to look around and catch sight of Him the way children look for their parents in the crowd at sports events. *Father, are You watching me? Are You getting all this?*

The Bible says that God is with us: "Where can I go from your Spirit? Where can I flee from your presence? If I go up to the heavens, you are there; if I make my bed in the depths, you are there."* We know He dwells within us.† This is amazing news, but in practice it doesn't always feel that way. Although it is comforting to hear that God is unconditionally present, it can seem like wishful thinking or an unattainable spiritual experience. I recall a well-meaning friend once asking me, "Faith, do you enjoy spending time with Jesus?" She proceeded to share her way of experiencing Him and just how amazing it was. Truthfully, I wasn't inspired. Instead, I was frustrated. It felt like she was dangling something in front of me that I could never have for myself. I didn't feel spiritual enough or, perhaps, chosen enough to have these sorts of experiences with God. When discouraged by the mysteries of His Presence, we assume that these special connections must not be meant for us.

We have always attempted to make sense of what we can't understand by creating ways to manage the mystery. The unknown is uncomfortable, and worshipping a God we don't

* Psalm 139:7–8.
† John 14:16–18.

fully comprehend requires faith, so we tend to presume things about Him without getting to know Him first. Sometimes it is easier to fill in the blanks with our own limited assumptions, kind of like when people gossip about others they barely know. Humankind has been gossiping about God for millennia, instead of humbly seeking Him and allowing Him to reveal Himself in His way. We see this in big ways throughout ancient history. Greek mythology reveals a rich tradition of gods who demonstrated human traits and relatable fallenness. Egyptian mythology oftentimes depicted gods who were part human and part animal. We tend to associate God with what we already know and experience. It is easier to devote ourselves to what we are familiar with than to seek Him through the mystery.

Circumventing the mystery in this way keeps us from truly knowing Him for who He is. Even though we may not be worshipping Zeus, the Greek god of the sky, or Amon-Re, the Egyptian god of the sun, we, too, may be filling in the blanks and creating our own portrait of God. Years of counseling Christians in the church has revealed to me that many Christians' initial image of God reflects a parent figure or another person who influenced them in their formative years. Even with Bible verses like John 3:16 memorized, Christians can still wrestle with the feeling that the God they pray to is like an abusive father or an emotionally distant sibling. Perhaps it is difficult to pray, because you see Him as the untrustworthy friend you once had or the critical spiritual leader you knew. We take the little that we know of Jesus and mesh it with our life experiences. It is our way of creating a narrative for a God that we don't have the full narrative for. The mystery is uncomfortable, and we have a history of putting God into a manageable box.

The dilemma of the Christian experience is that we are meant to know Him without seeing Him and trust Him without always feeling Him. Even if we do see things and feel things, we don't always understand them. Did Peter understand why Jesus was walking on water?* Did the disciples understand why Jesus cursed a fig tree before entering Jerusalem?† Did anyone understand what was going on while Christ hung on the cross as a condemned criminal?‡ It was a mystery at that time. Just as it is a mystery for the believer when hopes are dashed by a tragedy and when prayers receive no desired results. It is a mystery when the heart seeks the Spirit but feels nothing in the seeking. At the end of the day, it would be nice if it could be as simple as holding Him when we grieve or casually asking for advice over dinner with Him.

Wrestling with the Mystery

Exodus 24:17 says, "To the Israelites the glory of the LORD looked like a consuming fire on top of the mountain."

At Mount Sinai, God clearly demonstrated who He was and what He was up to. Moses had been going up the mountain to hear from God and back down to deliver His message to His people. They couldn't deny the sight of smoke billowing up from the mountain nor the shaking of the ground beneath their feet. Mothers must have held their babies tighter. The terror and magnificence they beheld were reminiscent of the plagues in Egypt. So, when Moses called the Israelites to consecration, they immediately obliged. When the prophet returned from the mountain to call for a wholehearted dedication to

* Matthew 14:22–33.
† Mark 11:12–14.
‡ John 19:17–30.

God's covenant, the people responded, "Everything the LORD has said we will do."*

But things began to get murky. Getting to know Him can feel like that. One day, you feel like you've figured Him out, and later, uncertainty manages to shake that confidence. Moses went up the mountain once more, but this time, he was immersed in God's Presence—literally! The people had never seen anything like it. A cloud covered the mountain, and Moses remained there for forty days and forty nights.† For more than a month, the Israelites had to wait. Nights came and days passed. Meals were eaten, and there was still no sign of Moses. The people became restless. Each day that passed chipped away at their certainty. The unknown was becoming a heavier burden. There was no clarifying message nor guiding sign—just mystery.

Like it was for the Israelites, the wilderness is where we struggle to understand who God is and what He is doing. It is where expectations aren't met and timelines are confounded. It is where hard work doesn't pay off and plans fail. Doors remain closed and losses outweigh gains. Discouragement seeps in because our devotion to Him doesn't seem to matter and His Presence feels far. Obeying Him feels like it's in vain. The wilderness of the soul is a spiritual desert where God doesn't seem to be showing up the way we want Him to. We have expectations about how God will act, but when those expectations are dashed, we are left with mystery. The Bible says that He is merciful, but our circumstances can feel merciless. Scripture says that He is abounding in steadfast love, but how come all we feel is abandonment and rejection? The mystery is the tension between biblical truth and our real-time experience.

* Exodus 24:3.
† Exodus 24:15–18.

Although the mystery of God may veil the things that we are looking for in Him, it surely does unveil the things that are within us. For the Israelites, it revealed much: a lack of trust, an affinity for the idols of Egypt, and the need for control, among many other things. It all took the form of a golden calf they created to worship, an effort to reclaim a semblance of security.* They did what we all tend to do when staying faithful in the darkness becomes too heavy of a burden. They turned away from the Presence and settled for a counterfeit.

When God doesn't meet your expectations and you are thrust from your comfort zone, what comes out of you? Some of us may not even realize we have stopped depending on the Holy Spirit because of a growing jadedness toward God. Those who are accustomed to living independently from Him will turn to something or someone else. When secret comforts and dark habits arise, they are typically easy to point out. However, we can also replace God without knowing it. When listening to His voice feels impossible, the voices of dynamic preachers become an alternative. When relying on Him for direct guidance isn't a part of our everyday lifestyle, we turn to religious culture to tell us how to behave. It is our nature to default to the familiar and settle for substitutes, because that is often easier than navigating the tensions of sitting in the mystery of His Presence.

Recognizing the Mystery

It is possible to experience friendship with God in the mystery, but it is first important to recognize when you are wrestling with it. The paucity of understanding and control can make us feel like something is subpar about us, that we are, perhaps, not good at this "believing in God" stuff. However, the mystery is

* Exodus 32.

normal, and recognizing what we are experiencing allows us to process it with faith. The following are some of the experiences with God that not only perplexed the Israelites in the wilderness but also perturb us today.

Waiting

Seasons of waiting can feel like rejection from God. The longer we wait for God to reveal Himself or move on our behalf, the more it feels as though He doesn't care about our urgent pleas. Although the Holy Spirit is the Helper, waiting for Him to do something or say something can make even the most dedicated Christian feel helpless. The silence after a great cry to heaven tempts us to question His goodness. Because seasons of waiting are void of control and clarity, they can leave us feeling vulnerable.

Friend of God, He is with you in the waiting. Not only is He with you, but His goodness is also actively at work as you wait. Romans 8:28 says, "We know that in all things God works for the good of those who love him, who have been called according to his purpose." Whether you are waiting for new career opportunities as your financial situation worsens, or for the right significant other as you go through another holiday alone, or for remission while undergoing medical treatment, God isn't twiddling His thumbs while apathetically watching. He is up to something—for your good and for His glory.

Disappointment

When we walk with Jesus, our lives aren't free of letdowns or bad news. Things happen in life that simply don't have a good explanation. It could be the way church leaders behaved or a betrayal by someone you trusted. After tearfully praying on behalf of a loved one, you could be seeing the opposite results from what you had hoped for. Perhaps what once felt like a blessing later felt like a curse, and it has left you wondering why God allowed it into your life in the first place. In fact, why does God allow us to meet certain people when they will cause great pain? Why does He allow us certain opportunities when they eventually lead to suffering? It is a mystery.

Disappointment tempts us to regret trusting in Jesus, because it can feel as though faith only guarantees hardship. Being wary about believing again is a very real experience that is often covered by polite smiles and small talk on Sundays. The sorrow of unmet expectations can infect our souls with skepticism and jadedness. In this sort of mystery, our limited understanding tells us that God stood us up. However, our limited understanding won't guide us to an intimate knowledge of His Presence.* Faith during disappointment is choosing to trade our limited understanding for trust. It isn't easy to trust Him when life disappoints, but it is childlike. In the end, it is childlike faith that allows us the grace to befriend His Presence in the mystery.

Suffering

Deep pain and extended periods of suffering expose any cracks or fragility in our faith in Jesus. For some, adversity will reveal whether we truly believe that God is with us. The Bible says that He is a God who will never leave us as orphans,† but our experiences can feel void of His Presence. For others, however,

---

* Proverbs 3:5–6.
† John 14:18.

the real stumbling block during the dark night of the soul isn't whether God is present. It is whether God is good enough to trust during our suffering. We may believe that Jesus is pure and holy, but is He worth following during trial and loss? Is He worth praising when He didn't stop certain misfortunes from barging into our lives? When agony takes its toll, we sometimes have little to no fight left to think the right thoughts or commit to the right Christian responses. In my time in ministry, I have walked with people through illness, divorce, and job loss who eventually confessed that it was difficult to acknowledge Jesus because it felt pointless. Thankfully, although pain can paralyze the soul, it can't push the Holy Spirit away.

The Presence of God doesn't guarantee the eradication of pain, but it does offer a peace that far surpasses our pain. To truly know Jesus is to be in the eye of the storm and remain content. Before you write this off as an optimistic platitude that can never work for you, remember that the apostle Paul said in Philippians 4:12–13,

I know what it is to be in need, and I know what it is to have plenty. I have learned the secret of being content in any and every situation, whether well fed or hungry, whether living in plenty or in want. I can do all this through him who gives me strength.

Yes, it is possible to be at peace even during times of need. Cultivating a genuine friendship with His Presence makes it possible. If you are intimately familiar with suffering in this season, may you seek to become even more familiar with His Presence. You do so by engaging with Him through honest conversation, which involves pouring out your heart to Him, then waiting in expectant silence as you make space to listen and receive His peace. Acknowledging what He's done and meditating on Bible verses can also raise your awareness of His Presence in times of suffering.

Mysticism

God is supernatural, so it's no surprise that the Bible is filled with mystical encounters with God. Jacob dreamed of a stairway to heaven, with angels ascending and descending on it.* The Israelites heard the voice of God through thick, billowing smoke from a mountain.† The apostle Paul spoke of a man in Christ who was caught up to the third heaven, and of this mystery, even he said, "Whether it was in the body or out of the body I do not know—God knows."‡ The supernatural is an undeniable aspect of God's nature.

Every friend of Jesus is called to be a mystic, to reach beyond intellect to know His Presence in the realm of mysterious love. King David was a mystic who depended on this deep knowledge of God's Presence, which you see in the way he was able to pray,

> One thing I ask from the LORD,
>   this only do I seek:
> that I may dwell in the house of the LORD
>   all the days of my life,
> to gaze on the beauty of the LORD
>   and to seek him in his temple.§

* Genesis 28:10–17.
† Exodus 19–20.
‡ 2 Corinthians 12:2.
§ Psalm 27:4.

David didn't just talk at God, but he experienced Him as well. You get there by loving Jesus and being open to what you receive from Him, while not prematurely deciding what you should or shouldn't experience in return. In settling for a knowledge of Him that makes sense to us, we create our own god rather than wholeheartedly yielding to the Holy Spirit.

It's so easy to reduce what it means to follow the way of Jesus to having well-considered Christian stances, consistent church habits, and established Christian tradition. It is easier because it requires no faith. Genesis to Revelation tells the story of a God who is meant to be encountered. It isn't enough to have head knowledge. We are meant to experience a relationship. When you commune with His Presence, allow yourself to be open to what you may sense or feel. However, don't unnecessarily pressure yourself with an inventory of experiences that you assume you should be having. No one particular experience is a prerequisite to having a beautiful friendship with Jesus.

Allowing Room for the Mystery

To enjoy His Presence, we need to become comfortable with mystery. Having space for your questions and being willing to be openhanded makes your relationship with God stronger. During Jesus's day, the Pharisees were supposed to know Yahweh the best. After all, they were teachers of His laws. When we hear the word *pharisee* today, it is a negative label, often used to describe a hypocrite. However, this group of teachers was once noted for their *akribeia,* a Greek word that means "exactness" or "precision."* It connotes a spirit of excellence due

---

* Kent L. Yinger, *The Pharisees: Their History, Character, and New Testament Portrait* (Eugene, Ore.: Cascade Books, 2022), 62.

to their refusal to miss the mark. They were experts in God's words and precepts. This way of life was rooted in the desire to preserve God's people from the corruption and compromise of the secular government that oppressed them. *Akribeia* was the manner in which they learned laws, recited Scripture, and followed traditions. Although Christian history recalls them in a negative light, they were originally a group of people that dedicated their lives to maintaining Israel's devotion to God.

Yet, when the Messiah came, they missed it. These leaders who retained so much knowledge with such exactness were incapable of recognizing the One whom all their laws were dedicated to. The God they studied about and taught on walked right past them, and not a word of praise escaped their lips. Instead, they resisted Him. They stood watch and criticized Him. In Matthew 12, the Pharisees accused Jesus of breaking Sabbath laws. This revealed they clearly didn't know the One who gave those laws in the first place. The Pharisees were flabbergasted as Jesus healed a man's hand before their very eyes. It made no sense. It didn't align with their knowledge of Sabbath laws, and Jesus didn't fit into their framework of thinking. They couldn't understand Him or control Him. This is a problem only for those who hold on to pride over intimacy with God. It was a mystery, but their stubborn arrogance kept them from being able to properly process the mystery with faith. Their standards, expectations, and self-serving agendas left no room for God's way. They assumed that this couldn't be God. When our hearts are filled with pride, knowledge doesn't help us befriend His Presence. Our ability to befriend Jesus depends not on how much we know but rather on how yielded we are.

The mystery demands a simple trust in God. It requires humility to surrender to this. We have the age-old tendency to minimize the mystery of God, instead of allowing Him to expand our thinking. Even as the worshippers of Jesus experienced the baptism of the Holy Spirit in the upper room and started declaring the wonders of God in foreign tongues, onlookers attributed it to drunkenness!* We don't get to hold Him to our standards and form Him according to our understanding. If intimacy with Him is what you long for, then you must be okay with admitting how much you don't know Him, even if you have led Bible studies or worship services in the past.

Someone who did make space for His mystery was the apostle Peter. It didn't come easy for Peter, though. In Acts 10, while communing with God's Presence, Peter saw an enigmatic vision and received an order from God to eat forbidden animals. I know—already this story sounds odd. Verses 11–13 say, "He saw heaven opened and something like a large sheet being let down to earth by its four corners. It contained all kinds of four-footed animals, as well as reptiles and birds. Then a voice told him, 'Get up, Peter. Kill and eat.'" Even without understanding Hebrew law and tradition, anyone would acknowledge that this is a strange thing to behold! It made no sense to Peter, so he refused the three times he was asked. And as he was pondering this mysterious encounter, a knock sounded on the door, and he was met by the very men that the Spirit had told him to expect. No five-step program or sermon could have coached Peter on how to handle the vision, the imagery, God's commands, and these strangers at the door. He just had to follow the leading of the Holy Spirit. The next day they set out for the home of a Gentile, Cornelius. Peter delivered the gospel to the Gentiles, although it was breaking Jewish law to associate

* Acts 2:1–13.

with them.* This moment opened the door to take the good news beyond the Jewish people to the rest of the world, changing the trajectory of the church forever. Imagine if Peter had refused to make space for the mystery in that hour! It was so illogical that Peter felt that it was righteous to resist it. Often we believe that for something to be of God, it must make sense to us according to our culture and our way of thinking. I wonder how often we resist His guidance and His blessings simply because they don't make complete sense to us.

Our response to the mystery reveals our secret attitude toward God. When the Israelites experienced the mystery of God in the waiting, they attempted to sidestep the discomfort of having to humbly use faith. Instead of allowing the tension of uncertainty and unanswered questions, they took matters into their own hands and created an alternate god that felt familiar. They wanted to serve a god they could control. Similarly, when the Pharisees faced the mystery of a Messiah who didn't fit their expectations, they chose their earthly knowledge and traditions over His Presence. They had no room for an infinite God because that would require them to lay aside their self-serving agendas.

Mystery is awkward to sit with, especially when God doesn't feel present and His ways make no sense. When you are under the torrent of one disappointment after another, it's hard to imagine what a loving God could possibly be doing. Sometimes He asks for your trust instead of providing you with perfect understanding. The discouragement may tempt us to turn away. And yet turning away would merely lead us to substitutes that offer counterfeit peace.

The existence of mystery isn't evidence of His aloofness.

* Acts 10:28.

Rather, it's a testament to His eternal nature. It means that He is greater than our ability to comprehend. If toddlers were offended by their first exposure to the world, they would never explore and ask questions, which is essential for them to reach milestones and grow to maturity. If marine biologists were discouraged by the blackness of the ocean floor, they wouldn't send divers and machines to explore the deep sea. If NASA scientists spurned the universe for how vast it is, they wouldn't pour billions of dollars into research to see a little farther into space. The mystery of God isn't a rejection, nor is it a result of a lack of proximity. Instead, it is heaven's red carpet rolled out for you to discover the pleasures and beauty of His infinite glory.

If you want to experience friendship with Jesus, you must be willing to relinquish any preconceptions that limit Him to what *you* believe He should be. To understand His Presence, you need to reconcile yourself to the tensions you face as you grow deeper in intimacy with Him. Openness and humility allow God to reveal Himself to you in rich new ways. Placing your limited and false beliefs on Him only hinders this beautiful friendship from blossoming.

Embracing the Mystery

The mystery of His Presence is an invitation to draw closer to God. To accept this kind invitation is to endlessly discover the height and depth of His love. It is a lifetime quest. Paul wrote to the Christians of Ephesus, "I keep asking that the God of our Lord Jesus Christ, the glorious Father, may give you the Spirit of wisdom and revelation, so that you may know him better."* How exciting that whatever we know of Jesus, it is possible to know Him better! We get there by embracing the mystery.

Everything we don't know about God means there is space for growing in knowledge of Him. Just like in human relationships. Every person we know has their share of mysteries as well. The man I knew at the altar on our wedding day isn't the same man I know today. My knowledge of my husband has grown over time. Year after year, the gift of covenant relationship has allowed me to unveil the nuances of his character, his heart, and his design. I know so much more of Dave today than I would have ever imagined when I met that eighteen-year-old in college. Although the early days were hyped with butterflies and fireworks, my knowledge of my future husband was two-dimensional at the start. He was just young, athletic, and funny! Today? My knowledge of my husband is deep. It is complex. And I am still growing to know him better.

The key to developing a healthy and real relationship with the Holy Spirit is to approach Him with great expectation and no agenda. I approach Him, knowing He welcomes me. I trust that He is available and present with me. But I don't have a specific expectation as to how I must feel or what I must receive. Can you imagine if we had agendas like that for the other relationships in our lives? It would be impossible to grow in intimacy with anyone if we demanded that they make us feel and think exactly the way we want when we are with them. We can't hold our faith hostage to human standards, refusing to believe in Him unless we experience Him in certain ways. Just like Brother Lawrence's quest, may yours be

* Ephesians 1:17.

simple and childlike. Although he didn't wish to be widely known, he was a mystic whose relationship with God captured the attention of prominent and educated Christians. And we can still apply his simple devotion to our complicated lives today. May the following encouragements—from the monk and me—help you take up the invitation of love that mystery extends.

Draw Close Anyway

You don't need much to draw close to Jesus. Brother Lawrence said, "Neither skill nor knowledge is needed to go to God."* You don't need to fully understand Him to access Him. You don't need special training to be with Jesus. You can still cast all your cares on Him. You can still petition Him for help. You can still listen for His guidance and turn to Him for comfort. Sometimes we get so aggrieved by our inability to understand that we forget He is present anyway. Even if He didn't do what you wanted Him to do in seasons past, He is still God. You can approach Him.

God never promised that you will have all the answers when you want them. However, He does guarantee His Presence. He is with you, whether you feel Him or not. It is the blood of Jesus that guarantees His proximity, not your understanding. We tend to overestimate the power of our understanding and underestimate the power of our choices. You can always choose Jesus.

James 4:8 says, "Come near to God and he will come near to you."

* Brother Lawrence, *The Practice of the Presence of God* (New Kensington, Pa.: Whitaker House, 1982), 21.

Let Love Lead the Quest

"An illustrious bishop of France" (as he was called) interviewed Brother Lawrence several times to eventually conclude that "God spoke directly to Brother Lawrence, revealing His divine mysteries to him because of the greatness and the purity of his love for Him."* Befriending the Presence of God has less to do with what you know and more to do with who you love. Instead of trying to figure out God, just love Him. And if you are feeling a paucity of affection for Jesus, try widening your awareness of His love for you. Take some intentional time to consider the gospel. Reflect on how He has blessed you thus far. Slow down and remember all the ways that He has been merciful to you. Meditate on the reality of His love. You can also dedicate every part of your life to Jesus, whether it be praising Him in your car or praying while you shop for groceries. Let the primary aim of your life be loving Jesus—not becoming a better person or racking up good deeds.

Dwell and Remain

Sometimes the tension of not fully being able to grasp God can discourage us from wanting to sit with Him for any longer than we must, similar to the way we scramble to find our way out of uncomfortable conversations. In the Gospels, Jesus was constantly being asked questions—approximately 183 in all.† Of these questions, He answered only a handful, and even fewer did He answer directly and clearly. Perhaps our faith is fortified not by clear-cut answers but rather by

---

* In Joseph de Beaufort, "The Life of Brother Lawrence," in *Practice*, 85.
† Martin B. Copenhaver, *Jesus Is the Question: The 307 Questions Jesus Asked and the 3 He Answered* (Nashville, Tenn.: Abingdon, 2014), xviii.

dwelling with Him while not being offended by what we can't comprehend.

Sit an extra five minutes with Him when in prayer. Meditate on a verse for just a little bit longer than usual during your Bible studies. Remain. When Jesus started talking about eating His flesh and drinking His blood, many of His disciples left.[*] The mystery was too perplexing, and the tension between what they did and didn't understand was too much. However, Peter said, "Lord, to whom shall we go? You have the words of eternal life. We have come to believe and to know that you are the Holy One of God."[†] Peter decided to stick with Jesus even when it made no sense to so many others. To stay with Him in the mystery is to acknowledge that He is God and we are not.

Turn to Scripture

The Bible is your greatest guidebook into the Presence of God. Whenever you feel as though you can't hear Him, turn to Scripture. If you are ever wondering what He thinks of you, read Psalm 139. If you are ever curious about His ways or His heart, try the epistles, like 1 and 2 Corinthians, Galatians, Ephesians, and Philippians. If you are struggling to find words for prayer, Psalms is a great place to find them. If you want to get more familiar with Jesus, try any of the Gospels—Matthew, Mark, Luke, or John. Even getting a devotional book with bite-size pieces of Scripture and reflections is a great start to developing an affinity for the Bible.

Reading the Word is a way to experience His Presence. Open those pages, and you will find a meeting place with the Holy Spirit. Greet Him with the first verse that you read. The

[*] John 6:48–66.
[†] John 6:68–69.

context of what you read may be ancient, but its revelations are timeless and eternal. Sitting with a Bible verse can lift the fog from your mind. It makes you available for the deeper things of His Presence.

Practice Sacred Assumption

There have been times when worshipping God would melt my every carnal thought and sentiment, and then there have been times when it felt like I was singing to dead air. I have spent hours sitting before God feeling absolutely nothing, and yet I have also had spiritual encounters that have marked me forever. We can't control our encounters with God. If we believe that He is close even when the atmosphere around us feels empty, then we will still come away from that moment in peace. This is the practice I call sacred assumption.

Sacred assumption is the way we bridge the gap between what we believe and what we are currently experiencing—with faith. Faith reminds us to assume good things about God. Assuming He is good while we are in the mystery is a choice to trust in His kindness and integrity. It is a refusal to create a false narrative of who He is, regardless of what the circumstances feel like. When we are in confusing and dark times, the greatest temptation is to latch on to narratives that speak ill of God.

"He's left me."
"He doesn't care."
"He's angry."
"He can't help."

Instead, practice sacred assumption.

"He's doing something good right now."

"He's for me, not against me."

"He's kind."

"He's with me."

Allow His Presence to tell you how to interpret the wilderness, instead of allowing the wilderness to tell you how to interpret God.

Dear Friend of God

We experience spiritual frustration when our longing for God meets with unsatisfactory results. Either the emotions you felt during worship were underwhelming, or the things you encountered during prayer were confusing. His Presence is mystical in nature because He is Spirit. Trying to control our experiences with Him is like grasping water with our bare hands.

I have witnessed countless people experience God in ways that I have yet to experience. I used to be envious of this. I thought I was less spiritual than they were or perhaps not repentant enough, until I realized that we are all different and are meant to experience Him in our own unique ways. As I focused on pursuing Jesus over pursuing experiences and encounters, my relationship with Him began to grow. The more I grew in this way, the less I needed to compare my experiences with others. Because He is with me in such a personal way, I wouldn't even expect others to have the same experiences, and vice versa. What a beautiful mystery!

The mystery of His Presence challenges our desires, agendas, and expectations. We must die to our flesh in order to navigate the mystery. Despite these challenges, navigating it is

44

simple. Love Him anyway. Allow that love to be your compass through the unknown. The good news is that the mystery of His Presence is meant to be unveiled. It isn't unveiled through striving or good works. You can't force answers or control the way He responds. Instead, the mystery is unveiled through a trust that can be found only in genuine friendship. Friends of God are endlessly discovering and rediscovering the goodness of His Presence. After all, the mystery isn't a closed door. Rather, it is an open invitation.

CHAPTER 3

The Sufficiency of His Presence

> The love of money was gone, the love of place was gone, the love of position was gone, the love of worldly pleasures and engagements was gone. God, God, God alone became my portion. I found my all in Him; I wanted nothing else.
>
> —George Müller, in Andrew Murray, *The Two Covenants and the Second Blessing*

What do you do when a preacher goes up to the stage and shouts, "God is good"? In many church traditions, the congregation instinctively and enthusiastically shouts back, "All the time!" As an itinerant speaker who visits many church congregations, I have always been surprised at how many people have this little tradition in their culture. It was likely ingrained in them when they were young, and to be honest, it feels good to shout it out! But do we truly believe it? Is the Presence of God enough, all the time, in all seasons, whether in victory or in trial? In theory, yes, He is. However, as most of us have likely experienced, the wilderness of the soul reveals what we truly believe.

Believing He is *good enough for you* changes everything.

Anyone can attest that God is objectively right in all things and probably better than the rest of us. Yet knowing this doesn't guarantee a vibrant spiritual walk that allows us to drink deeply of the well of His Presence. We must believe that He is good to us and for us. If we were convinced that God can handle our financial problems, familial crises, and mental health issues, then going to Him would make sense. If we genuinely believed that He has the power to help us and that He cares about our afflictions, then a life dependent on His Presence would be a no-brainer. It is imperative that we have an intimate and personal knowledge of His sufficiency, or we will find ourselves shouting "All the time!" at church while living a life independent of His Presence.

Believing He Is Enough

One of my daughters once came to me teary eyed because she had a small cut on her foot. Well, it was small to me at least. Yet, from a child's perspective, it was an injury that demanded immediate attention. Being both a pastor and a mama, I naïvely believed that this would be a grand teaching moment, so I said, "Should we pray over your boo-boo?" She looked at me with dismay and retorted, "No, Mommy! I need a Band-Aid!" I was taken aback. How could my Sunday school–attending child deny prayer? Had I failed her? Or perhaps she was expressing a common human experience. To her, Jesus was a good idea on most days, but when a little bit of blood was visible on her foot, He wasn't relevant. He wasn't the answer to the problem. She just wanted a Band-Aid.

We adults are like this as well. When we are at a church service, we sing those catchy songs that declare He is everything we need. During Bible studies, we say our amens to verses like Psalm 23:1: "The LORD is my shepherd, I lack nothing." But when the reality of life hits and we have our own bleeding foot, do we really believe that the Presence of God is enough?

By 2020, I had been a minister of the gospel for about fifteen years. But fifteen years of talking about Him and witnessing the amazing things He has done weren't enough to prepare me for what was about to transpire that year. As the globe shook under the impact of a pandemic, so did my trust in Jesus. Along with so many others in March of that year, my family of six began to lose everything we knew to the tumult of a locked-down world. We lost much and many in that season, and it hurt—deeply. At one point, with months of no income, we were on the verge of becoming homeless with four little children and a dog. It was a burden that was beyond my ability to bear. My mind was noisy with constant worry, and my body was fatigued with grief. So, I attempted to do the biblically sound thing and reach out to friends for support and good counsel. I poured out my lament to those around me, desperate for any revelation or guidance that could salve my heart in the midst of the crushing. However, most of the well-intended responses were something along the lines of "I'll be praying for you" or "God is with you." Oh, how that upset me! Those were empty words to me at that time, and after hearing them more than once, I began seething with anger. I recall thinking, *Telling me that He is with me isn't enough. I need a paycheck.* It was my version of "I need a Band-Aid!"

Chaos and trial place the limitations of our faith on display. Pain unveils our most honest perception of God, a perception that is sometimes unseen because it is buried beneath religious obligation and the theology we were taught. That year and the continued trials revealed the many cracks in my trust in the Holy Spirit. My faith had reached the end of its rope.

Turning to His Presence during crises feels naïve, even impractical, at times. Needs demand to be met, and pain demands to be dealt with. But the nature of our relationship to His Presence is contingent on how dependable we believe Him to be. Is He enough, or is our Sunday worship just optimism put into song?

In Philippians 4:19, the apostle Paul said, "My God will meet all your needs according to the riches of his glory in Christ Jesus." These were the confident words of a joyful prisoner who remained strangely content while in chains.* If I were to be honest, I would have difficulty being content in NYC traffic, let alone in prison for defending the gospel! Although he was being punished, he was overflowing with gratitude. According to him, he was "amply supplied."† He spoke of a God who didn't just care for his needs but abundantly met them "according to the riches of his glory." God's love doesn't just send you well-wishes from heaven. He meets your needs. And not only does He meet your needs, but He also goes beyond them according to the riches of His glory! To know Him means to also know His provision, help, strength, and guidance. The Holy Spirit is a sovereign, omniscient, omnipotent, self-existing person. He is supernatural yet personal, with a heart ablaze with compassion for you. And by the grace of Christ, He chooses to dwell with you, to be everything you need while you roam on this earth.

He is worth knowing—intimately, authentically, and passionately. It was worthwhile for Moses to take a break from tending his flock to approach a burning bush. It was the most important moment of his life, one that forever changed redemptive history. It wasn't a waste of time for Joshua to spend

* Philippians 4:11.
† Philippians 4:18.

years sitting with the Presence of God in the tent of meeting. He must have logged countless hours in that dimly lit space while conversing with Yahweh. Those hours prepared him to lead Israel into the Promised Land. Abiding in Him was also the way King David was formed and sustained for his reign over Israel. His psalms that we still recite today are proof that David spent his life singing to his own King, and he sang to Him even after moral failure and mistakes. Knowing God was also paramount for Queen Esther, who, in terror, turned to fasting and prayer before she dared to approach Xerxes about helping her people. Each of these biblical heroes encountered great problems, and they met those problems with His Presence. Throughout our existence, there has been only one truly worthy opponent of darkness and chaos, and it has always been the Presence of God. He is sufficient. Jesus isn't a good-luck charm, nor is believing in His sufficiency wishful thinking. He isn't just an intuition or positive energy. He is Alpha and Omega, the Beginning and the End, the Ancient of Days, God Almighty, King of Kings, Prince of Peace, and our Heavenly Father.

When you believe in the sufficiency of His Presence, you will be drawn to His company more than His blessings. A prayer life that is focused solely on asking for provision, help, and strength, without seeking God Himself, is transactional, not relational. That's more like a relationship we might have with our accountants. During tax season, we pay for a connection to an accountant so that our taxes are filed correctly. However, that is typically as far as the relationship goes, for we wouldn't think of spending an idle afternoon in the park with our accountants! We go to accountants for their skills and services, not for their company. God isn't our accountant. His companionship is of the greatest value. I recall a time when I opened the doors of the church building to spend the evening with the Holy Spirit, and I invited many of my friends to join me in spending time with Him. But I got asked, "What are we gathering to pray for?" to which I replied, "Nothing! We are just spending time with Jesus!" It took a moment for that to make sense to some. We don't need to have an agenda to go to God. Spending time with Him is the worthiest agenda.

Led and Fed by the Presence

The Israelites left everything they knew to start a journey to the Promised Land. They had only recently been unshackled from slavery. Even though their time in Egypt was oppressive, it was also predictable. They disdained the tyranny, but they were also familiar with it. They understood it. And now they were on their way to claim a land they had never seen while walking on terrain their feet had never touched. Nothing was foreseeable. They couldn't even predict where the next drink of water would come from. To say that there was uncertainty along their travels would be an understatement. However, instead of a battle strategy, a meal plan, or a map, what the Israelites received was the Ten Commandments etched in stone.* As you may know, the first four of the commandments describe how we are to love God—wholeheartedly and without contest with any other. The last six are His guidelines for how we are to love others. These Ten Commandments were how Israel was to remain in alignment with Yahweh.

Instead of directions on how to survive, the Israelites were given directions on how to abide in God! They didn't receive a step-by-step manual on what to do in "the vast and dreadful

* Exodus 20:1–17.

wilderness,"* with its natural threats and countless enemies. It was unlivable terrain that wasn't ideal even for a visit, much less for building a life and raising a family. How easy is it to respond to something like this by leaning on your carnal instincts to take what is yours in order to survive? By giving His people the Ten Commandments, God was communicating that His Presence was better insurance than hustling and scheming. The temptation in the wilderness was to succumb to the belief that God wasn't good enough. Was He actually able and kind enough to be their guarantor of the Promised Land?

Obedience proves that we trust in the sufficiency of God. The Israelites needed to believe that the One who was wise enough to outwit Pharaoh, powerful enough to split the sea, and kind enough to ensure they had plunder on their way out would be just as capable of walking them through this frightful terrain. Did they trust that He was enough to the point that they didn't require idols? Were they able to honor the Sabbath and rely on Him to sustain their lives while they rested? Were they able to look to Him for their needs rather than steal and kill? They wouldn't need to take from their neighbors if their hearts were brimming with contentment in God. When we believe that God is enough, disobedience is no longer necessary.

Yahweh desired that the Israelites would find satisfaction in His abundance and power. It is also His desire for us today. If God's people had truly believed that He was sufficient, they wouldn't have turned to their own devices to fulfill their desires. They would have had no room for self-reliance, idols, backup plans, or haughty grumblings against one another and against God. Any action or thought that contradicts His pre-

* Deuteronomy 8:15.

cepts is a declaration that His Presence is inadequate for protection, direction, and provision. It is evidence that we don't believe that He is capable of helping or kind enough to care. When we don't trust in God's sufficiency, we start doing things apart from His Presence and contrary to His ways. Just as Israel struggled with this in the desert, we struggle with this today.

The good news is as it always has been—God is God even when we don't trust Him to be. Despite the Israelites' stubborn lack of confidence in Yahweh, the wilderness journey revealed that He was always worthy of it. He fed them all. He guided every step. He preserved the lives of the young and vulnerable. Even amid the constant complaints and failures of His people, God proved Himself to be faithful by protecting the next generation and raising them to be strong enough to fight battles and claim their home in the Promised Land. Near the end of the forty-year journey, Moses commemorated God's faithfulness by saying, "Man does not live on bread alone but on every word that comes from the mouth of the LORD. Your clothes did not wear out and your feet did not swell during these forty years."* For forty years, Israel was led and fed by Yahweh. Although the Israelites persistently tripped over their doubts, the wilderness journey proved that He had always been enough. This is good news for those of us that have failed deeply in the wilderness. You may not have bravely praised Him in the struggle. You may have grumbled through the pain. You may have stayed up worrying about your plans. You may have turned to darker comforts that feel too shameful to bring up to your church leaders or, perhaps, even to God. It may be days or years since you last felt spiritually alive. Yet here you are, reading these words. Darkness didn't beat you. Take heart, Friend of

* Deuteronomy 8:3–4.

God. None of what you did in the wilderness made Him any less gracious and merciful. You can still trust Him.

Faith in His Sufficiency

As you grow deeper in your friendship with God, every season has a purpose. In our suffering, we know His comfort. In our failures, we know His grace. In our lack, we know His provision. In rejection, we know His loyalty. Although none of these valley seasons provide opportunities for self-advancement, they do provide deeper, richer revelations of who He is. The way we react to dark times often reveals what we believe the point of our lives actually is.

In 2020, my husband and I were trying to plant a church during a pandemic. That wasn't the original plan, but it became the plan. In order to start a church, on the most basic and practical level, you need people and money. We had neither.

For months, my husband and I held meeting after meeting. We vision-casted and threw barbecues. We made cold calls and even googled "church planting." We went through our life savings, something that we had hoped to put into a down payment for a house of our own. Sometimes we made an inch of progress, and other days we fell behind a mile. After a year of very little movement, I was vexed over what felt like wasted time and wasted resources. I was overwhelmed with a sense of failure and deeply scared about the future. One afternoon, I barged into my bedroom, closed the door, and said, "Jesus, I can't keep going on like this. You need to tell me how to get this done or how to let it go. It's one or the other because I'm at my wit's end."

Desperation pushed me to honesty, to acknowledge the truth that God had already seen in me. Like most confessions, it didn't sound pretty. It was faithlessness pulled out from the basement of my heart and presented on the table before the Holy Spirit. It was no surprise to Him. God is gracious enough to meet us in our honesty; it is merely surrendering to Him what He already knows.

In this time spent with God, He drew my attention to Philippians 3:8:

> I consider everything a loss because of the surpassing worth of knowing Christ Jesus my Lord, for whose sake I have lost all things. I consider them garbage, that I may gain Christ.

I read it, and quite frankly, it didn't seem helpful. I found myself responding, "Why are You trying to change the topic, God?" Sometimes when we feel this way, it's because we are the ones off topic. I wonder how often we miss what God is trying to say simply because we are fixed on the secondary things. Although I was uncomfortable with it, I sat in the mystery for a bit longer, and I made room for Him to address the tension, which He did by revealing this truth: My purpose was to know Jesus more through this. Planting a church was what we were called to do, but it wasn't our primary purpose.

For months, I had been forfeiting my friendship with God to attain results, but on that day, I returned to my Friend. Although I have always been with Him, I hadn't been aligned with Him. Recommitting myself to His Presence didn't mean that I neglected my daily responsibilities and became a recluse exclusively dedicated to prayer. Rather, it was a shift in focus, a change of priorities. I ceased to make Him a means to an end. He was the goal. He was the purpose. In the next few weeks, I responded to all the letdowns and setbacks with "Lord, today is still a meaningful day because my purpose is to know You." It wasn't always easy, but it was simple.

One day, my husband came out of his own prayer time, with faith in his eyes and a calm in his voice, to tell me that God revealed to him that we needed to start holding official worship services. And naturally, his wife, whose name is literally Faith, faithlessly laughed at the idea. "With what?" was my response. We didn't have enough people on our team to fill a living room, let alone a venue. All we had was a microphone stand with no microphone. We had no equipment to even hold a worship service. But we had very little left to lose at that point. So, we circulated an announcement on social media and started to invite everyone from friends of friends to grocery store workers. We planned to hold a worship service in a rented ballroom in a small local hotel. I figured I would just project my voice and we would make do. However, the week before the gathering, a pastor from Brooklyn gave Dave a call. They had recently closed a campus site and had a storage space filled with equipment. At that time the Holy Spirit, our Helper, inspired this pastor to donate two U-Haul trucks filled with equipment to us. We were given more than what we needed for a worship service. In fact, it was enough for a fully functioning church. When I heard the beeping outside my window as the trucks were backing into our driveway, I cried. Then I laughed, this time with gratitude. I thanked my Friend because His Presence was—and has always been—sufficient.

The Names of God

At the start of their wilderness journey, the Israelites officially knew God as Yahweh, which means "I am." Exodus 3:13–15 says,

Moses said to God, "Suppose I go to the Israelites and say to them, 'The God of your fathers has sent me to you,' and they ask me, 'What is his name?' Then what shall I tell them?"

God said to Moses, "I AM WHO I AM. This is what you are to say to the Israelites: 'I AM has sent me to you.'"

God also said to Moses, "Say to the Israelites, 'The LORD, the God of your fathers—the God of Abraham, the God of Isaac and the God of Jacob—has sent me to you.'

"This is my name forever,
    the name you shall call me
    from generation to generation."

Names matter in relationships, and the name by which we call someone reveals what we know about them. "I Am" is *ehyeh* in Hebrew, which is a conjugation of *hayah,* which means to "be" but also to "become." It is existence in action, an immanent presence. Before the plagues of Egypt and the emancipation from slavery, the Israelites already knew that God existed. However, when Moses arrived to lead them out of Egypt, it was time to know Him as the God who was immanently present, the God who would manifest Himself among them.

The journey from Egypt to the Promised Land may have begun with an introduction to Yahweh, or "I Am," but the gift of the wilderness was the continual discovery of God. The longer they walked together, the more Israel was exposed to other dimensions of His character. Along the way, they began to call Him by other names.

In Exodus 15:26, He was called "the LORD who heals
 you": *Jehovah-rophe.*
In Exodus 17:15, He was called "the LORD is my
 banner": *Jehovah-nissi.*
In Leviticus 20:8, He was called "the LORD who makes
 you holy": *Jehovah-M'Kaddesh.*

Israel's nomadic journey around the desert wasn't just a sad
story of problems and failures. Instead, it was a continual unveiling of God. Every trial and tribulation revealed another aspect of the Almighty.

Even when it feels like God is absent or failing to meet our
needs, He is still revealing Himself. Favorable circumstances
and feel-good emotions don't equate to His Presence. As Abraham stood on the mountain, shaking at the prospect of having
to sacrifice his son and risk his legacy, he discovered that God
was Jehovah-jireh: "The LORD will provide."* Gideon, while
hiding in fear of the Midianite people, encountered Jehovah-
shalom: "The LORD is peace."† Jeremiah, during a time of grave
corruption and failure, declared Him to be Jehovah-tsidkenu:
"The LORD is our righteous Savior."‡ David, who needed God's
guidance and care, called Him Jehovah-rohi: "The LORD is my
shepherd."§ The list could continue, for our God is infinite in
nature and sufficient in every way.

The wilderness of the soul will always point to God's sufficiency. Heavy pain invites a weightier Presence. Loss welcomes
His abundance. Even in failure, He forgives and remains with
us. We often mistake hardships as God's way of punishing our

* Genesis 22:14.
† Judges 6:24.
‡ Jeremiah 33:16.
§ Psalm 23:1.

flaws or forcing us to demonstrate godly character and endurance. It could even feel as if we are being sadistically tested for some unknown purpose by a cold God. When we process disappointments without faith, our hearts create false portraits of God. Yet, when we choose faith, we look up from the wasteland to recognize the One who is with us still. We begin to know Him in deeper, more intimate ways.

For some of you, He is . . .

The Lord who is with you in your loneliness.
The Lord who loves you in your failure.
The Lord who helps you unravel problems.
The Lord who gives you peace during chaos.

For my daughter several years ago, He was the Lord, the Provider of Band-Aids.

The Power of Remembrance

Remembrance is an effective tool when we struggle to feel that God is enough. You can go back as far as you can remember and acknowledge every blessing He has given to you, every time He has protected and provided for you. This may be difficult at first when you are in a season of deep pain. However, remembering the good that God has done is choosing to see Him in the unseen. You are never without the proof of God's Presence in your life. Taking the time to remember is choosing to recognize that proof, while complaining is choosing to ignore it. Complaining fortifies our unbelief and our distrust in God, for it is an intentional focus on everything that God hasn't done. It is the opposite of grateful remembrance, which is an intentional focus on everything that God has done. Not only does this help us believe that He is sufficient, but it also helps us *feel* that He is sufficient.

Moses said to the Israelites, "Remember well what the LORD your God did."*

Remembering Him exalts Him. When we exalt God, fear becomes illogical, although we may still feel its lingering chill. Even so, we gain the strength to resist its oppression. Anxious thoughts diminish God because they insist that God can't or won't help us. Remembering His ways and His works challenges these thoughts. Remembrance ushers our entire beings into the knowledge that He is and has always been sufficient. Try getting a fresh journal and making it a practice to recount every blessing that God gives you each day!

I always wondered why a general knowledge of His goodness didn't transform me as much as I thought it should. I felt guilty in the times when it wasn't enough for me to know that He is right about all things and deserves my trust. I didn't realize that the revelation I needed was not just that God is good but that He is also *good to me.* The difference may seem subtle, but the implications are massive. The fact that He is transcendent, holy, and almighty stirs up awe. But the revelation that He is immanently kind and accessible draws us closer. When we start to trust that God is good to us, it changes our hearts' posture as we approach Him. He is good to you and good enough for you. And that God wants to befriend you. Yes, you!

Dear Friend of God

The thing that stood out to me about Brother Lawrence was just how satisfied he was in Jesus. He discovered the gift of the

---

* Deuteronomy 7:18.

gospel and thoroughly enjoyed it like a child. Brother Lawrence didn't just believe in the sufficiency of God's Presence; he relished it. He trusted Jesus with every single detail of his life and gave himself over to Him with abandon. Reading his words, I felt like I was watching someone enjoy the most extravagant, hearty meal, but through a television screen. For years, I wondered how I could get to that place. He had given himself so wholeheartedly to Jesus that he said, "I began to live as if there were no one but God and myself in the world."* That seemed easier for someone living a simple, rhythmic life in a monastery centuries ago. I couldn't sit idly in the hope of having the same experiences one day. So, I embarked on my own journey with God's Presence, seeking Him in the midst of the jungle of my own life. After all, I, too, am His friend.

Ultimately, this journey made me realize at least one thing. The issue wasn't my external conditions. The gift that Brother Lawrence enjoyed wasn't given to him because of his choice of vocation and setting. It was a matter of faith. Now, before you roll your eyes and give up because of this grandiose church word, hear me out. By *faith*, I don't mean the enthusiasm to read the Bible or listen to Christian songs 24/7. It isn't an emotion or special ability. It is trusting that the Presence of God is sufficient for you—wise enough to guide you and good enough to help you. This trust can be found in your silence when you get bad news. It can be found in how you remain anchored amid chaos. It can be found in that sigh as you get up and do the right thing, even when you don't want to. That trust declares that although every bit of your flesh aches to do it your way, you choose to believe that He is good enough to turn to, to rely on, and to love. Your faith is a continual exercise of trust

* Brother Lawrence, *The Practice of the Presence of God* (New Kensington, Pa.: Whitaker House, 1982), 52.

in Christ's sufficiency. Your phone notifications can be buzzing. Your boss can be on edge. A loved one's health can look unpromising. Yet in the whirlwind, you can remember. Remember the friendship. Remember why you breathe. Remember what He has done for you up to this point. Then you are, in your own way, living as if there were no one but God and yourself in the world—because He is enough.

PART 2

Drawing Closer to
God's Presence

CHAPTER 4

Acknowledging His Presence

He is within us; we don't need to seek Him elsewhere.
—Brother Lawrence, *The Practice of the Presence of God*

Today we are blessed with more resources about the gospel than ever before. These days, choosing a gospel preacher to listen to is like choosing an avatar for a video game! There is a variety to choose from, and you usually pick the one that best reflects your preferences. You need a course on Christian dating? You can google it. You need help interpreting the Bible? You can stream classes. You need to activate your leadership skills? There are coaches for that now. You want to know your God-given calling? Pick a conference, any conference! However, despite all that is available to us today, there has been a significant decline in the number of practicing Christians and church attendees in the past two decades.* It seems that although they can be helpful tools

---

* "Signs of Decline & Hope Among Key Metrics of Faith," Barna, March 4, 2020, www.barna.com/research/changing-state-of-the-church.

and guides, access to Christian information and personalities doesn't guarantee a growing relationship with God.

As a pastor, one of the most frequent laments I hear from people is that they feel far from God. It's a difficult burden for those who attribute this feeling of distance to their failings and unworthiness. Some of us feel like it's impossible to befriend Him because of the great chasm that our depravity and unholy thoughts create. Even churchgoers find themselves struggling to feel close to Jesus, so they attend Sunday services as polite acquaintances who maintain a semblance of proximity through the traditions of Christianity. But spiritual vitality is dependent on our intimacy with Jesus Himself. As long as we keep sidestepping the Presence of God, we will miss the point of the gospel. We must cease to settle for His shadows and actually seek His face.

The place to start in befriending Jesus is to work on growing an awareness of His Presence. If the purpose of our lives is to know God, then the first step to fulfilling our purpose must be to learn how to acknowledge Him.

Grumbling in the Wilderness

When we aren't in close fellowship with His Presence, we tend to resort to grumbling through the wilderness seasons of our lives. Just as a teenager mumbles under his breath after a disagreement with his parent or an employee mutters in resentment after leaving her boss's office, grumbling is possible when distance is created. In these scenarios, the teenager doesn't feel connected to his parent, while the employee has walked away from her boss. Where there is strife, there is grumbling instead of communicating, rebellious murmuring instead of leaning in for understanding. Having been a youth pastor for twelve years, I have heard my fair share of grumbling from students.

However, rarely was I ever meant to hear this grumbling. Several times, I heard irritated comments about camp rules or certain youth group leaders in the ladies' bathroom when teenage girls were unaware that I was in a stall close by. The awkward hush was immediate when I, the youth pastor, came out of the stall and showed up at the sinks. The moment they were aware of my presence, the murmurs ceased. In a similar way, we tend to be immersed in our discontent and doubt when we forget just how close the Holy Spirit is.

Israel knew that Yahweh existed, as evident in their cries to Him during their plight in Egypt.* However, calling out to someone for help and acknowledging them like a friend are different dynamics. Although He was visible in the plagues that shook Egypt and broke their shackles of slavery, the Israelites weren't close to God the way Moses was. Thus, when things got tough, they grumbled. In fact, they had taken only one step out of Egypt when the grumbling began.

> Was it because there were no graves in Egypt that you brought us to the desert to die? What have you done to us by bringing us out of Egypt? Didn't we say to you in Egypt, "Leave us alone; let us serve the Egyptians"? It would have been better for us to serve the Egyptians than to die in the desert!†

> If only we had died by the LORD's hand in Egypt! There we sat around pots of meat and ate all the food we wanted, but you have brought us out into this desert to starve this entire assembly to death.‡

* Exodus 2:23–24.
† Exodus 14:11–12.
‡ Exodus 16:3.

Why did you bring us up out of Egypt to make us and
our children and livestock die of thirst?*

As weak and ungrateful as Israel seems, this bitter murmuring
is relatable. We do it to gain a false sense of power in powerless
situations. In their vulnerability, the Israelites sought someone
to blame, thus charging God with sadism and Moses with ter-
rible leadership. Grumbling is the coping mechanism that we
instinctively use during difficulties, instead of lifting our gaze
to the one true Helper.

The Israelites' grumbling also reveals how easily we question the value of our allegiance to God while in the wilderness.
Although the Israelites were walking on answered prayers, the
desert exposed their fair-weather devotion as they began to ro-
manticize their past slavery in Egypt. When life with Jesus is
tough, a common temptation is to consider your own way of
doing things as a simpler and better alternative. Your soul will
say something like, "Okay, God, if You're not going to get me
out of this, then I'm going to get out of it myself." This is when
we begin to ignore the Holy Spirit and lean on our own intuition. When grumbling turns to action, we cultivate a spiritual
independence from the Presence that leads to dependence on
other people and things. When the faith walk is difficult, you
may find yourself wishing for the things that you left behind to
follow Jesus, like that toxic relationship, unhinged drinking
habit, or apathy to God. People choose the chains of unhealthy
attachments and dark comforts during wilderness seasons because they are, at the very least, predictable. Just as the Israelites
saw a return to Egypt as a solution, we mistake slavery as freedom because it offers a sense of control, even though it also
tethers us to our fears and carnal desires.

* Exodus 17:3.

It's easier to rebel than to acknowledge Him, to stew in our discontentment and unbelief than to turn to His Presence. How many times have we resorted to complaining, blaming, and lamenting on our own or with other people without ever once presenting our problem to Jesus? How many times have we posted about it on social media rather than praying to Him in a secret place? Grumbling merely punishes our souls with a sense of greater distance. But, Friend of God, you can make a holy trade today. You can trade the grumbling for friendship. Although it may feel unnatural at the start, you can meditate on the following truths as you combat your grumbling:

- *He is with you:* "Where can I go from your Spirit? Where can I flee from your presence? If I go up to the heavens, you are there; if I make my bed in the depths, you are there."*
- *He knows what He is doing:* "As the heavens are higher than the earth, so are my ways higher than your ways and my thoughts than your thoughts."†

Before spending another half hour brooding over pent-up bitterness, worrying over an outcome, or mindlessly scrolling on social media to escape your problems, try reading these two passages and sitting on these truths for a while. Consider their implications for your life. Meditation on God's truth unites your mind, body, and spirit and allows the whole of you to be fully present with Jesus.

---

* Psalm 139:7–8.
† Isaiah 55:9.

The Gospel Is the Gift of Himself

Throughout biblical history, God's solution to every impossible problem was to offer Himself. The cry of Moses at the start of his time as leader, before taking even one step toward Egypt to emancipate his people, was "Who am I that I should go to Pharaoh and bring the Israelites out of Egypt?"* It was the fearful question of someone desperately aware of his own shortcomings. God didn't respond with affirmation or encouragement. After all, it is never God's agenda to coddle our insecurity. Instead, God has always overshadowed our insecurity with this age-old response: "I will be with you."† The only worthy answer to all of Moses's needs and wants was Yahweh Himself. Even at the end of the wilderness journey, just before the Israelites' conquest of the Promised Land, God said to the newly appointed Joshua, "Have I not commanded you? Be strong and courageous. Do not be afraid; do not be discouraged, for the LORD your God will be with you wherever you go."‡ God's Presence was the gift and the guarantee. To His people, who continually drifted away and rejected His Presence, God time and time again reached out and said, "I will be with you."

The essence of the gospel is that God gave us Himself. We can easily miss this. There are several perks to becoming a Christian, which we talk about frequently in the church. You get a spiritual community. You get to experience the freedom of forgiveness. You get hope for the future, a sense of calling. You get inspiration and encouragement from Christian books and

* Exodus 3:11.
† Exodus 3:12.
‡ Joshua 1:9.

music. However, at the end of the day, the point of the gospel and the very heart of Christianity is to personally know Jesus—a gift that we can ignore even on a Sunday.

If you believe the gospel, you must also believe that He is with you. The gospel would be powerless without His Presence. He was and still is the only real solution to the depravity of humankind. Our perfect connection with His Presence was severed in the garden. Every dark corner on this earth is a result of this severance, for none of the evil that we see around us is a result of God's design. We invited it by walking away from our Creator. But God, being God, took it on Himself to mend what we broke and to bridge the gap that we created. He removed the separation between Himself and humankind by laying down His life. When we rejected God, He offered Himself anyway. So, those who embrace and follow Jesus today receive the gift that He so humbly suffered for us to have—the gift of His Presence. The gospel undoes the blunder in the garden. The cross guarantees your proximity to God. Any feeling or thought that tells you otherwise is a lie to distract you from this truth. Because He humbled Himself to endure an execution that should have been ours, He is yours to keep forever. The gospel allows us to acknowledge Him and not beg for Him, to experience His Presence rather than strive for nearness.

God Is with You

When I was a youth pastor, a student of mine experienced God in a radical way during a Friday night gathering. Christianity had been his parents' faith until that moment. He was an intelligent young man, and for years, he had many questions about theology and church tradition. Yet on that one momentous evening, he opened his hands during worship and began melting in love. Tears rolled down his face, and he was too caught up in God's Presence to even care to wipe them away. After the worship service was over, he ran to me with a glowing countenance, and this six-foot-tall teenager was ecstatically jumping up and down. He had encountered Jesus, and he was overflowing with energy, joy, and questions—lots of questions! As a spiritual newborn, he was trying to make sense of his new relationship with God. He wanted to stay in this state forever. As we were waiting for the after-church-service pizza in the cafeteria, he asked, "So, what do I do from now? Just . . . pray?" I will never forget the way he asked this: "Just . . . *pray*?" He sounded dubious, like he was thinking, *Is that it?* Could a seemingly ordinary thing like prayer really be the means by which he continued to flow in this river of life? He was expecting grand gestures to keep reaching toward God Almighty. It was wild for him to believe that Jesus simply remained with him, merely a whisper away—like a friend.

There are different levels at which you can know someone. You can know someone by name, as a casual acquaintance. You can also know someone as a colleague or a neighbor. However, if you have the privilege of going beyond this, you get to know someone as a friend. This opens the door to a different level of familiarity and intimacy. The closer you get to someone, the more exposed you are to their thoughts, their perspectives, and their desires. It is an honor to know anyone in this manner. It is the greatest honor of our existence to know God in this manner. For the Israelites, the holy of holies, located in the innermost part of the tabernacle, was the place where God could be known in this way. The holy of holies was where His Presence was, and it was behind a veil, not accessible to just anyone.

What God made inaccessible to others, He made accessible to a friend. When Moses entered the tabernacle, God spoke.* Moses heard the voice of God, and they had regular conversations there. It must have been a closeness like no other. Not only was this friendship valuable to Moses, but it was dear to God as well. In defense of His friend before his jealous siblings, God said of Moses, "With him I speak face to face, clearly and not in riddles; he sees the form of the LORD."† The Hebrew phrase for "face to face" here literally means "mouth to mouth." What intimacy! The man who once trembled before a burning bush was now God's closest confidant on earth.

You can have this kind of closeness with God too. Thanks to Jesus, the holy of holies is no longer behind a curtain. We don't need a high priest to be a mediator, because Jesus became the ultimate mediator for us.‡ There is no more veil. There are no more varying levels at which we can know God. We are the tabernacle, and the holy of holies is within us.§ The blood of Jesus did that. Through His life on earth, Christ eliminated the need for curtains and shadows. We no longer need animals, incense, and formalities to access His Presence.

The One in the burning bush. The One who parted the sea. The One who descended in smoke and lightning on Mount Sinai. The One who sent manna each day. Almighty God, undiminished, is now within you. The gospel doesn't claim that you get increasing increments of Him over time. Neither do you get less of Him just because you go through a bad season.

* Numbers 7:89.
† Numbers 12:8.
‡ Hebrews 9.
§ 1 Corinthians 6:19.

There isn't a lower-grade version of Him you get because you are a lesser-performing Christian. If any of this were true, it would be an insult to the Holy Spirit. You don't need to beg Him to come to you. He is already there. There is no more need for penance, for earning your way back into His favor. You can never lose what you couldn't earn in the first place.

John 14:17 says, "He lives with you and will be in you." To know Him—intimately, authentically, and passionately—you must first know that He is with you. Consider where you are right now, exactly where you are as you read these words. Whether you are in your room or in your car, He is right there with you. He just saw you fidget. He can hear you breathe. He can see every worry or gripe that crosses your mind. You must acknowledge this because you can build no friendship with Him unless you are first convinced of His nearness.

The Holy Spirit Is Loyal

When I became pregnant for the first time, I remember how surreal it felt to see those double lines on the pregnancy stick. My husband and I were in our early twenties, and none of our friends had children yet. I didn't physically feel my daughter, nor did I know her. Yet my life called for some drastic changes. After doing a bit of research online, I realized that I had to give up all my favorite things! No more third cup of coffee, no more frequent sushi runs, no more sweating in saunas—just to name a few. I was endlessly complaining those first few months of pregnancy.

Then, one evening, I felt a strange flutter. When it happened again, I realized it was my daughter's kick. I gasped and cried out, "Oh, you're really here!" It is amazing what just one little encounter can do to someone's perception of reality. It hit me in that moment that there was a living being within me, pure and innocent. Even if I denied her and ignored her, she would remain there. Even if I refused to change my lifestyle and ingested all the toxic things that could harm her, she wouldn't just get up and leave, for we were bound by blood. This revelation shifted the way I experienced my love for her. It also made me want to change and live a better lifestyle, for whatever I did mattered to her as well! Whether or not I acknowledged her existence didn't change her proximity to me. However, it did change the way I related to her. Acknowledging her allowed me to forge a connection and feel her presence, not just physically but emotionally as well.

And so it is with the Holy Spirit! A pregnant woman is pregnant even when she doesn't feel it. Whether she is at work or asleep, she is still with child. In the same way, the Holy Spirit, who resides within you, remains with you. Your friendship with Him begins the moment you accept grace and salvation, because the Holy Spirit begins to dwell within you. His Presence isn't based on your behavior report card. He doesn't associate with you according to how good you are at praying. Your access to the holy of holies within you was secured by Jesus.

Thinking that any false step or mistake could create distance from the one you love is draining. Any relationship that starts there is void of rest because it will feel as though your identity and security are always hanging by a thread. If you deeply mistrust Jesus's consistent and persistent Presence, then you aren't enjoying the gospel as He intends! This mentality is based on faulty theology and doesn't reflect the God that the Bible testifies to. Jesus isn't a flaky friend. He isn't a spouse who packs up and leaves. Our Heavenly Father isn't a parent who never returns home. He doesn't toy with your mind or play with your emotions. He is the embodiment of pure devotion. Don't forget this fact—not only is the One who is with you good, but He is loyal as well.

Scripture says that the Holy Spirit can be grieved and quenched.* He has emotions. Our ways do affect Him. He is a witness to our every thought and gesture. He can hear the comments we make under our breath. He can see the way we treat our waiters. He is a witness to our breakdown in the bathroom in the middle of the day. The Holy Spirit isn't aloof. He is present and aware.

And He always remains.

In James 4:4–5, the author reprimanded believers by saying,

> You adulterous people, don't you know that friendship with the world means enmity against God? Therefore, anyone who chooses to be a friend of the world becomes an enemy of God. Or do you think Scripture says without reason that he jealously longs for the spirit he has caused to dwell in us?

The words here are strong. Adulterous? Enmity? Enemy? These things are enough to make anyone walk away from another person. However, never does it say in this passage that He leaves. The most loyal friends are the long-suffering ones, the ones that remain in the tension and process the disagreements. Anyone can walk away the moment expectations aren't met. But the Holy Spirit, despite our rejection or betrayal, remains with us. Even on our worst days. The blood remembers what Jesus has done, even when we forget. The Holy Spirit is loyal. There is no separation. There is no distance.

* Ephesians 4:30; 1 Thessalonians 5:19.

You don't need to re-earn His Presence every time you fail or demonstrate weakness. Instead, you need to acknowledge Him. You don't have to strive for His favor and attention. Pursuing a genuine friendship with Jesus isn't as arduous as searching for long-lost treasure. He is yours and you are His. Allow the relief of His forgiveness to give you freedom from your past. Savor being wanted so extravagantly by your Father. Take advantage of having access to heaven's assistance wherever you are. Appreciate having His listening ear every time you speak to Him.

The Power of Acknowledgment

In the first week of our marriage, Dave and I were sitting down to have a takeout meal in our new apartment. As we were unpacking the bags, I noticed that there were no utensils. Instinctually, I went into the kitchen to grab a fork for myself and returned to the table without a second thought. My husband stared in dismay and blurted out, "What about me?" As a newlywed, I wasn't used to considering the other in the home. Because I was more accustomed to living alone, I didn't yet have the habit of acknowledging the one who was now my forever housemate and partner. Although he was perfectly capable of grabbing his own utensils, I realized in that moment what the lack of acknowledgment can do to a relationship. Acknowledgment forges intimacy, while the lack of acknowledgment can sever it.

A skill that every friend of God needs is consistent, intentional acknowledgment of His Presence. Acknowledgment gives permission for closeness. Giving someone the title of "friend" has no impact on your life unless you are willing to acknowledge their existence. You must make room in your life to consider them, connect with them, and grow in deeper knowledge of them. Acknowledgment is a choice to be aware of someone and allow them to affect your very being. Those that want to be affected by the Holy Spirit must be willing to recognize His Presence even in the mundane moments of their lives.

Ways to Acknowledge His Presence

Acknowledging Jesus is a powerful choice we can make at any moment. When we allow ourselves to take a break from focusing on what we are doing and who we are with, we can turn our gaze to Jesus. You can incorporate this in all that you do, for Proverbs 3:6 says, "In all your ways acknowledge him" (ESV).

It could be as simple as saying, "Good morning, Jesus," the first thing each day. We are so quick to grab hold of our phones or glance at news headlines before we acknowledge Him. In the elevator, you can adore Him and confess, "I'm grateful to be with You, Lord." You can pause while responding to emails in the middle of the afternoon and consider His Presence. Mealtimes are great markers during the day to refocus on Him. You can acknowledge Him while on a train or sitting on the floor folding laundry. You can do this no matter what season of life you are in.

If you are struggling with ways to acknowledge God in your day-to-day, you can try these practical means.

Adoration

When you adore someone, you choose to appreciate who they are and savor their goodness. I recall that the moments when I felt the most connected to my children were when I would just stare at them while they were asleep. I would fawn over their plump cheeks and be attuned to their breathing. I would touch their tiny hands and fondly remember the precious things they had done that day. These are some of my most cherished memories with them.

Prayers of adoration involve intentionally gazing on Jesus, allowing yourself to be immersed in who He is and what He has done. In prayer, it is easy to default to recounting our disappointments and burdens, which leaves us feeling far from Him. Adoration challenges this disconnection and opens the door to intimacy.

If there is anyone in the Bible who knew how to adore God in any season, it is King David! His words are a great place to begin. Here is just one example:

> I will extol the Lord at all times;
>   his praise will always be on my lips.
> I will glory in the Lord;
>   let the afflicted hear and rejoice.
> Glorify the Lord with me;
>   let us exalt his name together.
>
> I sought the Lord, and he answered me;
>   he delivered me from all my fears.
> Those who look to him are radiant;
>   their faces are never covered with shame.
> This poor man called, and the Lord heard him;
>   he saved him out of all his troubles.
> The angel of the Lord encamps around those who
>   fear him,
>   and he delivers them.

Taste and see that the LORD is good;
blessed is the one who takes refuge in him.*

Inclusion

Involve Him in everything, even in the things that feel trivial
and mundane. A true friend isn't someone who is merely aware
of your Sunday traditions. What often discourages us from developing a rich friendship with God is that we compartmental-
ize our relationship with Him, separating it from other parts of
our lives. You may be leaving Him out of things that matter to
you, mistakenly thinking that they are irrelevant to Him. It
could be the traffic you are stuck in on the way to work. Perhaps it is your growing list of errands. Or it could be someone
in your life that vexes you, and although you know what you
must do, you are paralyzed by frustration and bitterness. Jesus
died and rose again for *all* of you, not just for the supposedly
spiritual parts of you.

First Peter 5:7 says, "Cast all your anxiety on him because
he cares for you."

He cares! So, include Him in all things. Share with Him
your frustrations as you make decisions. Admit your fears while
you are in financial planning. Share with Him your delights
while doing your hobbies. Acknowledge Him when you are
cooking. Give Him a nod when you're in between meetings.
Pour out your anxieties at His feet every evening, for He cares.

Dedication

First Corinthians 10:31 says, "Whether you eat or drink or
whatever you do, do it all for the glory of God."

* Psalm 34:1–8.

"Whatever you do" is a phrase that challenges us to surrender every aspect of our daily rhythms to Him. Once we give our lives to Jesus, they are no longer our own. He gave His life to love us eternally, so it makes sense for us to give Him ours to honor Him and magnify His name. In the Bible, anyone and anything that was dedicated to God belonged to Him. Honor Him with your work. As you put gas in your car, dedicate the moment to His glory. Even as you face an unpleasant conflict with someone, you can quietly yield that moment to God to do with it as He sees fit.

To dedicate your life to God also means that His will and way are your priority—even over your own goals and plans. It may not always be easy, but it will always be simple—to live for Him over anything else. Brother Lawrence once said, "Let us often remember, my dear friend, that our sole occupation in life is to please God."* Dedicate everything to Jesus. When you are in the habit of loving Him in all that you do, there is no meaningless moment. Everything becomes eternally significant when it is used to love Jesus.

Dear Friend of God

The most significant thing you can do at this very moment is to acknowledge Him. Let's try this together right now. Clear your mind. Yep, all of it! You can't hear from God if you are filling in the blanks for Him. Set aside all that tends to clutter that headspace—the to-do list, the worries, the pressure points. Just let go and make space within you. If it helps, breathe deeply and close your eyes. Turn on your awareness of His Presence. This alone may be a struggle if distracting concerns or painful

* Brother Lawrence, *The Practice of the Presence of God* (New Kensington, Pa.: Whitaker House, 1982), 48.

burdens are stifling your ability to shift your awareness toward His Presence. You don't have to stuff these things down or ignore them. This could harden your heart even more. Instead, just bring these things to Him. You can even imagine yourself bringing your sorrow and worries to His feet like a child would to a gentle father.

After quieting the clamor of the world, breathe in that growing awareness of His Presence. If other thoughts intrude on this moment, don't get hung up on condemning yourself about it. Don't get frustrated if you aren't good at this right away. This is a holy practice that will eventually get easier. It isn't limited to devoting a certain amount of time to Him. Rather, it is about raising your awareness of His Presence in every scene of the day. At the start, you may need a controlled environment such as a comfortable space with minimal distractions and, perhaps, some worship music in the background. Some find it easier to be aware of His Presence outdoors in nature—hiking, surfing, or taking a slow walk in the park. As you bask in the sun or feel fresh wind on your face, you can be aware of His Presence there too. If you are wrestling alone in a quiet room, you can change your posture to embody your intentions by kneeling or lifting your hands. If you find it difficult to empty your busy mind, turn your attention to the following scripture:

Where can I go from your Spirit?
   Where can I flee from your presence?
If I go up to the heavens, you are there;
   if I make my bed in the depths, you are there.
If I rise on the wings of the dawn,
   if I settle on the far side of the sea,

even there your hand will guide me,
  your right hand will hold me fast.*

As you discover what works for you, you will be increasingly attuned to the Holy Spirit. And as you continually acknowledge Him, you will be aware of His Presence even amid chaos and storms.

---

* Psalm 139:7–10.

CHAPTER 5

Accessing His Presence

The purpose of prayer is to reveal the presence of God equally present all the time in every condition.
—OSWALD CHAMBERS

Years ago, I received a guitar as a birthday gift. It was a gorgeous instrument given to me by my husband when I was just learning how to play. I would have never imagined that I would own a brand-new Taylor guitar. It's the type of guitar that serious worship leaders and experienced guitarists use—far more legitimate than the knockoff I got from Amazon to practice on. However, I will be painfully honest and admit that I never fully utilized this guitar. I hardly touched it and was barely able to play chords beyond A, D, C, and G. I had this beautiful instrument, but I rarely accessed it. Just as it would be unthinkable to have a Ferrari only to keep it in the garage or have a billion dollars just to forget it in the bank, it would be a tragedy to carry the Presence of God and never access Him.

God is with us always, but every relationship requires intentionality. For some of us, the Holy Spirit is a roommate that we see occasionally, perhaps briefly in the mornings or on Sundays. Yet this is like having a sip of water at the start of the day and at the end of it. You may survive, but you will be desperately dehydrated. Dehydrated Christians can find themselves attending events, meeting the right standards, and being surrounded by other Christians, all the while never fully engaging with Jesus. However, the privilege of practicing His Presence is blood-bought and precious, and you will never know true spiritual vitality without accessing it.

I experienced this one day when I was struggling with guilt as I was driving. My heart was racing with a sense of doom, replaying my missteps and feeling too ashamed to even speak to God about any of it. I considered going on a fast or committing to something—anything—to whip myself into shape so I could get myself back into His good graces and make myself feel better. Religious guilt is an oppressive experience. It tells you that there is something you should do or say to earn your access to Jesus. After a few more minutes of thinking how I could figure this out in my own strength, I felt the Lord speak to me: "Faith, why don't you just thank Me for My grace?" It sounded too good to be true, so my mind began fighting it. Was I really hearing Jesus, or was I unconsciously trying to self-soothe with positive thinking? However, upon weighing the biblical accuracy of what I heard, I realized that God was challenging the dysfunction in my view of our friendship. My access to Jesus can't be taken from me because of my weaknesses or mistakes. There is no religious activity or sacrifice that can convince Him to turn His favor my way. Faith must be the straw through which I receive this grace daily. He was good news when I first came to salvation, and He is still good news for the rest of my imperfect time on earth. So, I began to thank

Him for His forgiveness and for His unconditional love and kindness. Truthfully, it was awkward at first because it felt undeservedly easy. Is God really that accessible? Thanks to Jesus, yes. Yes, He is. Hebrews 4:16 reminds us, "Let us then approach God's throne of grace with confidence, so that we may receive mercy and find grace to help us in our time of need."

Accessing Versus Controlling

If you want to access His Presence, the posture of your heart matters. We can mistake access to God as the ability to control God. Without realizing it, we may be approaching Him as His clients instead of as His children. The difference can be seen in your agenda, desires, intentions, and expectations. Children rely on the parent to set the agenda. A client, on the other hand, determines the agenda and expects it to be followed. Your posture is evident in how you react to God when you don't get what you want in life. Whenever your expectations aren't being met, it is an opportunity to do a heart check. If we think God will follow our agenda, we expect specific results after our prayers "in Jesus's name." When we feel as though we have fulfilled our Christian duties, we expect things to be fixed after an "Amen." Consequently, we see happiness and fulfillment as the proof that He is with us. Yet, to enjoy the gifts of His Presence, we must humbly accept that He doesn't exist to meet our expectations. We know that we are choosing access over control if our friendship with Him is more important to us than having things our way.

Jesus understood this when He was in the Garden of Gethsemane, moments before His arrest. He was in great distress at the prospect of the cross. His execution was imminent, and it was going to be painful and unfair.

Matthew 26:39 recounts, "Going a little farther, he fell with his face to the ground and prayed, 'My Father, if it is possible, may this cup be taken from me. Yet not as I will, but as you will.'"

Even the Son of God was willing to allow His desires and preferences in that moment to die in the Presence of God. Jesus understood that He was able to freely make requests while trusting that His Father would decide on the ultimate good. Our prayers can indeed move Him, but they don't manage His movements. There is beauty in this. If the direction of our lives isn't up to us, then we are free of the burden of control. We know that we are accessing the Presence when we find ourselves in a place of surrender and peace. As the saying goes, we "let Jesus take the wheel." If someone else is at the wheel, we can rest in the passenger seat while enjoying the views. Surrendering our agenda to God is no punishment. Rather, it is freedom.

When we attempt to control His Presence, we hold our faith hostage until we see our desired results. A refusal to choose Him over our agenda will always hinder our intimacy with Him. He receives our requests, but we must also trust His final verdict. As you enter His courts, you will be met with grace and unconditionally loved. It isn't unreasonable for Him to ask that you love Him as He is in return, even if His ways differ from yours. When you take this trust fall, you are taking a deep dive into enjoying His Presence, because you are no longer in bondage to your agenda.

This was a hard truth for Simon the sorcerer in the book of Acts.* Before he believed and was baptized, he practiced magic and was known as "the Great Power of God." He had the people of Samaria wrapped around his pinkie because he had

* Acts 8:9–24.

power and a reputation. However, once he believed in Jesus, he was introduced to someone greater than himself—the Holy Spirit. This was new for him. He saw the works of His Presence, but he didn't know the Presence personally. He was amazed at how the apostles were able to make things happen by laying hands on people and saying prayers. It was a greater power than his, and Simon saw something in the Holy Spirit that he wanted to wield himself. Yet, instead of surrendering to Him, he tried to buy the power of the Holy Spirit with money. He didn't desire to seek His face. Instead, he wanted access to the work of His hands.

Several things happened here with Simon the sorcerer that may resonate with many of us who are wrestling with the difference between accessing His Presence and attempting to control His Presence.

Simon Couldn't Let Go of His Agenda

Although he called himself a follower of Jesus, he was still trying to fulfill his self-serving desires within the Christian context. He lived for power and control, and he couldn't let that go. He chose his agenda over God's Presence.

Simon Sought the Things of God Instead of God Himself

For Simon, friendship with Jesus wasn't the goal. He had other dreams and aspirations that took precedence over intimacy with the Holy Spirit. He missed the point of being a believer. People can be enthralled in the moment of salvation and then be distracted by the pursuit of power and provision. Although these are God's blessings, they aren't God Himself. Simon the sorcerer was seeking merely the shadows of His Presence.

Simon Never Went Directly to God

This is the sobering reality of Christianity. You can be around so much spiritual activity while never actually developing a personal relationship with God Himself. You can be inspired by the greatest testimonies and can be around Christians all day long while still never speaking a word to Jesus personally.

Jesus isn't magic. He won't fix every problem at the sound of an "Amen." He isn't pressured by our fears. He will walk when we shout at Him to run, because He isn't late nor is He anxious. He is all-knowing and all-powerful. To access the gifts of His Presence, you need to be willing to wade in the mysterious waters of holy love.

To sit with Him when you want to act.

To trust Him when things don't go your way.

To love Him in the absence of instant gratification.

Jesus isn't magic. He is so much more than that. He is God. Accessing Him begins by leaving our agenda at the cross. Beloved Friend, it is natural to want a lot of things. I sure do. Ambitions and desires aren't bad things to have, as long as they remain secondary to the pursuit of friendship with Him. Although it is great to have goals, may you hold on to them with a light grip. Although making plans is good, may you be open to Jesus changing them. A heart that is yielded is one that will know Him very well.

Practicing the Presence of God

We receive the Holy Spirit at salvation, but constant communion with the Holy Spirit takes practice. The day you decide to live for Jesus, you begin to exist as one with God, as 1 Corinthians 6:17 says: "Whoever is united with the Lord is one with him in spirit." You are His temple. You carry Him. However, practicing the Presence takes you from co-existing to continual communion. It is an exercise of the soul that develops our awareness of and connection to the pleasures of knowing Him. It is what Brother Lawrence dedicated his entire life to. He said, "I still believe that all spiritual life consists of practicing God's presence and that anyone who practices it correctly will soon attain spiritual fulfillment."[*]

Practicing God's Presence doesn't need to end with your dedicated time of prayer. It never needs to end. It is a lifestyle of keeping the lights on for Jesus, no matter what you are doing or who you are with. You know that you are getting better at practicing God's Presence when you are more aware of His thoughts than other people's opinions. It develops spiritual muscle that allows you to tap into His peace no matter who isn't responding to your text or what plans fell through. Knowing Him is more than just a positive idea or a religious attitude. Forging that connection allows you to experience Him as tangible—real.

Psalm 16:11 says, "You make known to me the path of life; you will fill me with joy in your presence, with eternal pleasures at your right hand."

The beauty of practicing the Presence is that it is simple, and if it ever gets complicated, you only have to bring it back to its intended simplicity right away. It isn't about concentrating on Him to the point where you are distracted from your responsibilities. It is not an interruption of your day but rather an enrichment of it. It is like grocery shopping with a loved one. You enjoy the time spent together, all the while still checking off your list. Practicing the Presence isn't a competition be-

---

[*] Brother Lawrence, *The Practice of the Presence of God* (New Kensington, Pa.: Whitaker House, 1982), 32.

tween Jesus and the rest of your life. It is developing the habit of keeping your spiritual eyes open and your mind available to Him. The connection between God and His friend can be as natural as breathing.

Tools to Access His Presence

Let's get more practical here. It starts with simple interactions. Despite how basic this sounds, don't undervalue the way it can radically transform your life! I can talk to you about a delicious meal and describe every ingredient. I can even list the meal's nutritional benefits and provide the details of how it was prepared from farm to table. You can know everything about this meal, but it will do nothing for you to simply know these things. You must eat it for yourself. The pleasure and benefits of this meal can be experienced only when you grab a fork and try it. Similarly, you can go through your wilderness journey knowing in your mind that He is good, but it will just be an optimistic thought unless you engage with Him yourself. Practicing His Presence isn't just a mental exercise; it is a spiritual exercise requiring action.

Just begin. The best time to pursue friendship with Jesus will always be now. There isn't one particular method you need to adhere to. Interact with Him casually throughout the day, but also set aside intentional moments. Allow yourself to approach Him in ways that are natural to you, but also be deliberate in practicing the Presence.

May this also be a gentle reminder to performance-driven friends of God that it is "practicing the Presence" and not "performing the Presence." You aren't trying to prove something or earn anything. The following are reliable ways to practice the Presence.

Scripture

As I mentioned before, read the Bible often. If you want a close relationship with God, be familiar with His words. Bible reading isn't research, nor is it like completing a reading assignment in a textbook. Every page in the Bible is a place to meet with the Holy Spirit. Dwelling on His words is a way to sit with His Presence. The Bible will be your ultimate guide as you navigate the ebbs and flows of His Presence.

Psalm 1:1–3 says,

> Blessed is the one
>   who does not walk in step with the wicked
> or stand in the way that sinners take
>   or sit in the company of mockers,
> but whose delight is in the law of the LORD,
>   and who meditates on his law day and night.
> That person is like a tree planted by streams of water,
>   which yields its fruit in season
> and whose leaf does not wither—
>   whatever they do prospers.

According to this psalm, the blessed one isn't somebody who understands everything the Bible says or chooses the right translation. It is someone who meditates on God's written words and delights in His truth. The difference between meditating and reflecting on the Bible is that reflection is investigating meaning whereas meditation is making space for truth and dwelling in it. Everyone meditates on something. You may be meditating on your plans for the day or what your boss thinks about you. You may be meditating on your weight and body image or that one comment left on your social media page.

Whether it is God or not, something is taking up room in your mind. May it be Jesus.

Meditating on the Bible allows you to acknowledge God, consider Him, and make room for Him to minister to your heart. You may not always feel it, but it is nourishing your soul. It is a violent disruption and eradication of toxic ways of thinking.

Prayer

Pray wherever you are. Use your own words, and bring those prayers into every space that you enter. The apostle Paul advised the Christians of the Thessalonian church to "pray continually."[*] In other translations, this command is "Never stop praying" or "Pray without ceasing."[†] This can be daunting for those who feel pressured to engineer moments that are just right for prayer. I used to think that the rhythms of motherhood were a hindrance to my prayer life because I didn't have predictable times to isolate myself in a secluded area. However, what motherhood really did was set my prayer life free! Because I was no longer able to find that precious hour or two to escape into a secret place to talk with Jesus, I began to pray wherever I was. I no longer had to find time for the secret place, because the secret place began to stay with me. When people ask me how, as a mother of four and a pastor, I find time to pray, I often say that I never really stop!

When you begin to intentionally practice His Presence through continual prayer, it may not feel like you're doing it right. Prayer isn't necessarily a nonstop verbal transaction between you and God. Imagine spending the day with a loved

---

[*] 1 Thessalonians 5:17.
[†] 1 Thessalonians 5:17, NLT, ESV.

one. If you are with someone who sees you, knows you, and unconditionally loves you, you don't always have to spend the day with locked eyes and be deep in conversation. On the contrary, if you are with someone you trust, there will be natural moments in the day to pause, to divert your attention to other things, to casually share thoughts, to vent, and to listen. You can communicate with some people without even having to say a word! This is how it is while you are accessing His Presence through prayer. You can be pouring out your heart one minute and listening to His guidance the next. You can be groaning in grief or silent in contentment. You can be bringing up topics to seek His perspective, or you can be thanking Him for that amazing parking spot you just landed at the mall. You are always touching heaven when remaining in prayer through life's ebb and flow.

Praise

Praise Him. Whether you sing it, recite it, or shout it spontaneously, praise Him frequently. Where you praise Jesus, there God is. Yes, it is really that simple.

Psalm 22:3 says, "You are holy, enthroned on the praises of Israel" (ESV).

Your songs of praise enthrone Him, and He is seated on your thanksgiving. He inhabits your hums and hymns. Opening your mouth to exalt God is like setting up a chair by your side and inviting the King to sit with you. Your exaltation of Jesus welcomes His Presence.

Praise is also a way to access Him when overwhelmed by opposition. Praise invites God's victories into our lives. Not only is our praise an invitation for the Holy Spirit to commune with us, but it is also an invitation for Him to move before us.

Throughout history, praise has been a weapon of warfare because it declares that the battle belongs to God and that we belong to Him.

In 2 Chronicles 20, Jehoshaphat used praise to invite God's Presence into his battle. He was facing an impossible situation: A vast army had assembled for the sole purpose of destroying his people. However, at the temple of the Lord, in front of the assembly of his people, Jehoshaphat said, "We have no power to face this vast army that is attacking us. We do not know what to do, but our eyes are on you."* This is what praise does. It deals with the impossible by fixing our eyes on His Presence. Knowing they would soon be marching to battle, Jehoshaphat and his people bowed down in worship. And as they approached the battlefield, Jehoshaphat sent worshippers to the head of the army.

They sang, "Give thanks to the LORD, for his love endures forever."†

While they sang, the Lord set ambushes against their enemy and fought for His people. The key to their victory was accessing His Presence through praise.

Community

Not only are we called to practice the Presence by ourselves, but we are called to practice in community as well. We are able to access the Presence of God in special ways with brothers and sisters in Christ. When you observe the great outpourings of the Holy Spirit throughout redemptive history, you will notice that they are preceded by unified gatherings of people intent on knowing Him and loving Him more deeply.

* 2 Chronicles 20:12.
† 2 Chronicles 20:21.

By gathering to seek His face, a community of believers takes practicing the Presence to a whole new level. In Acts 2, the Holy Spirit came upon a prayer meeting in a way that had never been seen before—tongues of fire and exuberant praise in different languages. However, what preceded this move of God was 120 believers gathering each day to pray in an upper room. This happened again in Acts 4, when the believers heard about Peter and John's arrest. In their fear and uncertainty, the community raised their voices in prayer. What happened afterward was supernatural. The Holy Spirit shook the place, and each person was emboldened to speak the word of God with courage! When a community accesses His Presence together, they release a movement of the Holy Spirit that affects the environment around them.

The purpose of the church isn't just to help us become better people and give us inspiration each Sunday. No, the purpose of the church is to gather and seek His face. Today many are painfully aware of how fallen religious leaders and institutions can be. However, we don't gather simply because we trust in pastors or because we feel seen within the church's four walls. No, the glorious purpose of the church is to be a spiritual family that practices the Presence of God together and ultimately shares Him with the world. I wonder if the vitality of certain church communities wanes not because they lack programs and funding but simply because they do Christian activities without ever practicing the Presence of God.

Work

For Brother Lawrence, one of the most effective pathways to intimacy with the Holy Spirit was fulfilling his day-to-day responsibilities. He believed that "our actions should unite us with God when we are involved in our daily activities, just as our prayers unite us with Him in our quiet devotions."* Work doesn't make us strangers to Christ if we use it as an opportunity to work with Him and for Him. We do this by . . .

- conversing with Him as we do the work
- asking Him for the grace to do the work well
- doing everything out of love for Him
- thanking Him once the work is done

The spiritual thirst of a Christian can easily be quenched by the ordinary routines of life. Yet every mundane activity and chore can be a touchpoint for glory if we do it for Jesus. What makes a moment supernatural isn't the absence of the natural. Rather, it is the inclusion of the Holy Spirit. Our friendship with Jesus isn't in competition with what is before us. Just because we are wrapped up in a meeting or on the phone with the insurance company doesn't mean that we can't commune with Him. Every little thing you do can be a love letter to God. Let's not mistake the hustle and bustle as an absence of the Holy Spirit, for even in these moments, His glory within us never dims.

You can access His Presence naturally—and dare I even say casually—throughout the day, and the above tools are meant to be used in a way that is authentic to you, whether you are a student with a flexible schedule or a worker on the graveyard shift. During His days on earth, Jesus did everything while continuously abiding in His Father, and this intimacy was unbroken by the demands of life. In addition to this, Jesus did indeed set aside time to devote to prayer.

Mark 1:35 says, "Very early in the morning, while it was

* Brother Lawrence, *Practice*, 23.

still dark, Jesus got up, left the house and went off to a solitary place, where he prayed."

Moments to retreat with God are opportunities to enrich your continual access of Him throughout the day. Are you a bad friend to Jesus if you fail to close the door on your roommates or wake up early enough to pray before the hustle begins? No. Your proximity to the Holy Spirit is determined by the blood, not your schedule or circumstances. However, just as long, private conversations are important for friends and just as quality time at the dinner table is important for families, there is value in concentrated times with God. They allow you to use these tools to intentionally dwell with Him and drink from the well more deeply. Whether you call it a quiet time, a daily devotional, or a morning prayer, these flexible terms describe the moments when you offer a sacrifice of time and attention. Here, your heart has the opportunity to be fully present. Your worship can be focused and intentional. You have time to delve deeper into Scripture so that it can equip you for the day. You can intercede with fervor. Ultimately, time away with God fortifies our everyday access to Him. It isn't a prerequisite to having a friendship with Jesus, but it is a valuable means to enriching it. When done right, your conversations and interactions don't end once you say "Amen" and close your Bible. Your friendship comes with you wherever you go.

Going Deeper: Finding Your Secret Place

There is no limit to how rich our friendship with Jesus can become. To know the deeper pleasures of His Presence, we must offer deeper parts of ourselves. Before a tabernacle was even set up in the middle of Israel's encampment in the wilderness, the Lord spoke to Moses face-to-face in the tent of meeting, a designated spot a distance away from the main camp. Then when Moses would leave to go back to the camp, Joshua, his aide, would remain to dwell with God. Joshua stayed in God's Presence, and he did this continually.

Exodus 33:11 says, "The LORD would speak to Moses face to face, as one speaks to a friend. Then Moses would return to the camp, but his young aide Joshua son of Nun did not leave the tent."

No one on earth will ever know what happened between Joshua and Yahweh in the tent of meeting. What did it feel like? What were the topics of conversation? What wisdom was imparted in those precious moments? I also wonder what Joshua confessed to Yahweh in that tent. What burdens must he have released there? There were no cameras to capture any of the experience for an Instagram audience. It remains a secret. After all, secrets are meant to be between friends.

This man who frequently remained in the secret place of devotion was chosen for public service. Joshua rose up to lead Israel after Moses's death, and it was under his leadership that Israel finally walked into the Promised Land. However, before any of that came to pass, Joshua spent decades under Moses's leadership, aiding him and trailing his steps. But during this earlier stage in Joshua's life, the real preparation was the time he spent in the Presence of God. Sitting. Dwelling. Tarrying. Abiding. Similarly, the time we spend with the Holy Spirit isn't to be reduced to an item on a checklist. What makes a secret place is not its location but rather the honesty and humility that we bring to God. In this place, our bitterest tears and darkest confessions are not only welcomed but also met with mercy.

Deuteronomy 29:29 says, "The secret things belong to the LORD our God, but the things revealed belong to us and to our children forever, that we may follow all the words of this law."

Yes, God has secrets too. There is so much more to know about Him than what is already written in hymns and sermons. Deeper things are His to reveal to those who are close to Him. Even Jesus shared more intimate knowledge with His disciples when the crowds went away. We pay for VIP passes at concerts and conferences to gain the inside scoop, a closer view, and exclusive details. If our Lord offers a backstage pass to His throne room, isn't it worth our attention? We spend hours listening to celebrity gossip, professionals on podcasts, or polarizing news reports. What if we more often turned our hearts toward Jesus to gain heavenly, eternal insight?

Dear Friend of God

I woke up this morning, and my first instinct was to check my phone. I had multiple texts, some related to family and some related to work. I then scrolled mindlessly on social media apps only to realize that I had yet to even acknowledge the Holy Spirit, who was with me right in that moment—my patient and loyal Friend. Although I try to make it a habit to acknowledge Him before I do anything else, my human flesh sometimes doesn't realize the glory that it thirsts for first thing in the morning. I felt a shadow of guilt creep up, but I didn't allow it to distract me further from His grace. I simply went to sit down with my Heavenly Father in the living room. However, as I sat there, my heart felt heavy with concerns and burdens, and my mind raced with distractions. Today, for some reason, I couldn't fix my eyes on Jesus. Instead of reprimanding myself, I simply presented my concerns before Him. Intimacy can't be instigated by shame or condemnation.

Intimacy demands authenticity. This morning, I had no strength to approach Him "the right way"; I just did it in the most genuine way. I presented my weakness, and He met me with grace. Even in our earnest pursuit of His Presence, we can still make it about following a formula. No, Friend, it is your yielded heart that pleases Him. Jesus defeated death so that you can have the things of heaven right now and for the rest of eternity. All the help and comfort you need in your wilderness season is available to you in this moment. Just begin. Approach Him with confidence. Approach Him continuously. Heaven waits for you.

CHAPTER 6

A Presence-Centered Life

To think that we must abandon conversation with Him
in order to deal with the world is erroneous.

—Brother Lawrence, *The Practice of the Presence of God*

My spiritual journey began at the age of six, but it wasn't until I was sixteen that I gave my life to Jesus. During those ten years, I had sporadic moments when I felt close to God, but at sixteen, it became clear to me that I wanted to dedicate my life to Jesus. It's a moment I will never forget. My mother, who had become a devout Christian by this time, saw fit to send me to a Christian youth camp in Mexico. I am not sure why I never questioned it, but I flew to San Diego and drove a couple of hours south of the border with a group of people I had never met. On that first night, I was uncomfortable, homesick, and completely embittered about being there! However, on a cool desert evening, the pastor preached the gospel to us in a way that made me realize that I had never made a conscious decision to follow Jesus. Until that moment,

I had thought that I was at the mercy of God just showing up in my life when He saw fit. For the first time, I realized that my relationship with Him began with my choice. I remember the moment I said yes to that call to salvation and experienced the baptism of the Holy Spirit. It wasn't something that just happened in my mind, nor was it a mere physical experience. It was all-consuming, and every dimension of my being was shaken. What was once an empty, broken heart trying to fix itself before God became a cup that overflowed. I fell in love with His Presence, and my taste for the world was utterly ruined after this taste of heaven.

Like many others, I faced a steep learning curve after I was saved. I left the Christian youth camp excited to take this newfound joy back to my family and to my school. I thought that change would come naturally to me because I was so enthralled in that moment. As a sixteen-year-old familiar with Christian rules and ways, I knew changes like turning from toxic habits and letting go of bitterness were expected now that I had become a Christian. This youth camp had inspired me to want to do good and be good. Yet it took a mere week at home in my everyday reality for discouragement and failure to dampen my passion, and I no longer felt close to Him. That exhilarating feeling that had supernaturally consumed me was gone, and for years, I strove to make up for what I felt was missing. Often I would settle for a stale devotion to Jesus, not because I didn't want Him but because I was too tired of trying to fit Him into my life. The contradiction was that, despite my belief in Jesus, I was still living for myself.

A friendship with God may begin with salvation but flourishes within a Presence-centered life. It is a life that has room for the companionship and leadership of the Holy Spirit. Engaging God like an extracurricular activity or an obligation tends to cultivate a weary devotion because it fails to conjure genuine spiritual vitality. Compartmentalizing the secular and spiritual parts of our lives causes us to constantly strive to balance the two. It's no wonder that busy Christians sometimes feel like bad Christians and that burnout happens as we try to compensate for what we lack spiritually. A Presence-centered life isn't filled with Christian activities. Rather, it is filled with Christ's Presence in all our activities.

Encamped Around His Presence

Imagine waking up one day not knowing where you will be by the end of it. You wake up in a pitched tent with minimal comforts because you aren't sure when you will have to break it all down and pack up to leave again. You peek outside to see where the glory cloud is. When you look toward the tent of meeting, you see the cloud hovering without moving in any direction. God isn't giving any directive to go anywhere, at least not yet. Perhaps you won't be traveling today after all. The children will be glad of it. Then you remember that you must prepare the morning meal before the family wakes, so you venture out to look for the manna that appeared with the morning dew, food from heaven. You count how many people need to be fed, and you gather the amount you need for that day alone, remembering Yahweh's direction. There are no pantries to store leftovers, but no matter since manna never lasts for more than the day it is given. Over breakfast, the conversation is about the latest announcement that Moses made after his personal meeting with God. You notice that the water supply is low, and you wonder when the next opportunity will be to replenish it. It is impossible to plan these things. You wonder if other people are also in need of water and if Yahweh is aware of this need. Then you recall the last time the people grumbled about this, and it didn't end well. You remember who He is and what He has done. Then you hear the announcement. The cloud is moving. It is time to break camp and start walking. Yahweh has communicated that you have been here long enough.

This was life in the wilderness for the Israelites. Every step, every meal, and every plan had to come from God. Their existence demanded total dependence on Him. It wasn't about building a life or discovering oneself. The agenda was set, and everyone was called to the same thing—to know and follow Yahweh. They couldn't even store meals for the next day except before Sabbath. Each morning, they had to wake up and look for the cloud of God or listen for an announcement about His directions. Imagine that as a lifestyle—waking up each morning to seek His Presence and to hear His words!

Numbers 9:17 says, "Whenever the cloud lifted from above the tent, the Israelites set out; wherever the cloud settled, the Israelites encamped."

Israel's life was centered on the Presence of God. Imagine a typical living room space. When you walk into the room, there is usually a television or, perhaps, a coffee table. More often than not, every chair and sofa is pointed toward this object. It is where the eye naturally turns and where the attention of the room is typically fixed. Israel was a living room where everything was pointed toward the tabernacle, the dwelling place of the Presence of God.

Numbers 2:2 says, "The Israelites are to camp around the tent of meeting some distance from it, each of them under their standard and holding the banners of their family."

The tribes set up camp in a certain order, and each pitched their tents under their flag. A leader was also appointed to oversee each tribe. When the Israelites left Egypt, there were six hundred thousand men on foot, and that number didn't include women, children, and livestock.* Traveling on this scale over the course of decades is a miracle in and of itself. My husband and I have trouble coordinating a road trip with four children. Forget leading a nation around for forty years! However, this was made possible because their lifestyle was centered on the Presence of God. In fact, the times when they failed were when they turned from God in disobedience. From Yahweh came the strategy, the strength, and the direction to not only travel through the wilderness but also grow as a nation within it. This is the power of a Presence-centered life.

The Presence-Centered Life Today

Occasionally my husband and I have date nights, and they are truly a special treat for us as parents of four children and two dogs. However, if our relationship were defined by our ability to fit in these special date nights, it would be a rocky relationship to say the least. We would feel extreme pressure to make sure that these date nights didn't fall through, and if they did, then we would feel a guilt-driven need to make up for lost time. Thankfully, this isn't the case, because we have built our entire lives as one. Our home is a space we chose together. Our children's schedule is something we collaborate on with both our ministries and our personal needs in mind. When we cook, we consider each other's palate and aversions. I am not trying to fit my husband into my life, because we have built a life where we have space for each other. Now, once you choose Jesus, you, too, are tasked with building a new life. If you merely attempt to sprinkle a bit of Jesus into days that serve

* Exodus 12:37.

you and you alone, you will always feel like you have to be re-earning intimacy. What would it look like for you to build a life with the Holy Spirit?

What we make room for is what we are building our lives around. For some of us, this is easily discernible, and for others, it may require honest reflection. Here are some guiding questions to begin that process:

1. What is the first thing you think about each morning?
2. What drives your everyday choices?
3. What inspires your goals?
4. What determines the way you manage your financial spending?
5. When you make plans, what is most important to you?
6. What do you pray about the most?
7. What preoccupies your thought life?

Your answers usually point to your version of the television in the living room. If you want to take the practice of the Presence of God from an extracurricular activity to a lifestyle, befriending Him must be what you center your life on. Even if you devote an hour in the morning to prayer, you could still be spending the rest of the day focused on earning favor at work. The way you dress, exercise, and talk could be centered on the hope that people will think about you in a certain way. You could add another Bible study to the week, but that doesn't change the fact that your eyes go to your phone screen every thirty minutes to check the latest updates on social media. A Spirit-filled life is also a Spirit-led life, and a Presence-centered lifestyle is how we get there.

He Wants More with You

I remember having coffee with a college student one day, and we spent an hour catching up on the wonderful ways her life had flourished since I last saw her. She glowed as she talked about all the job opportunities she was getting and the wonderful young man she was dating, and she also mentioned that there was a church back on campus that she visited once in a while. I said that was wonderful to hear, to which she replied, "Yeah, I don't really pray to God, but I know for sure Jesus is with me." She smiled at the thought of it—a God that was hovering over her life, watching over her steps. She was content with the idea of Him being nothing more than a guardian angel, perhaps even a good-luck charm, as she went about her life the way she wanted to. It was good enough for her. However, it didn't occur to her that there was so much more available.

God doesn't just want to co-exist with Christians like neighbors who share a street but never a meal. If Yahweh were okay with co-existing with humankind, then He would have sent Adam and Eve away from the garden and left it at that. The Bible would have ended at Genesis 3. Thank God it doesn't. Today we have a thick text of historical narrative, poetry, prophecy, songs, laws, and so on—all testifying how God kept speaking, reaching, intervening, and working to re-establish friendship once again. It is because He wants more with us. To dwell with us in abiding, intimate communion has always been His desire.

Before the wilderness journey began, He was the God who showed up in the burning bush, the plagues, and the parting of the Red Sea. Before the tabernacle was built, God was present with Moses in a pitched tent far from the camp. However, once the tabernacle was built in the center of the Israelites' encampment, God dwelled among His people again for the first time since the garden—but, this time, in the wilderness.

God said in Exodus 25:8, "Have them make a sanctuary for me, and I will dwell among them."

Even at our worst, He pursues us. What mysterious love that God desired to dwell with His grumbling, vulnerable, failure-ridden people in the desert. His fierce desire for us isn't contingent on our goodness or even the quality of our faith. He wants us because we are His to want. How amazing is it that He hasn't hated us when we have disregarded Him. It isn't just an obligatory love, nor is it charity for our poor and wretched selves. He is the Hound of heaven* and the Lover of our souls. He is pleased to pursue us.

First Corinthians 1:21 says, "Since in the wisdom of God the world through its wisdom did not know him, *God was pleased* through the foolishness of what was preached to save those who believe."

He was *pleased* to save you! He chose to make the sacrifice because He couldn't bear to spend eternity without you. Centuries of rejection didn't stop Him. Friend of God, you are wanted. You were worth the cross. Jesus endured execution so that He can dwell with you, not from a box like the ark of the covenant nor from a room full of curtains like the tabernacle. He wanted a friendship with you that couldn't be stolen or lost. So, He sealed it by bleeding for it and giving us the Holy Spirit to guarantee it.

God is passionate about our closeness. It matters to Him greatly. Just as we flinch when someone speaks to us in a sharp tone or get heartbroken when a loved one gives us the silent

* Francis Thompson, "The Hound of Heaven," Oxvision Films, accessed February 11, 2023, www.houndofheaven.com/poem.

treatment, God can feel the distance of our hearts. Isaiah 29:13 says, "These people come near to me with their mouth and honor me with their lips, but their hearts are far from me. Their worship of me is based on merely human rules they have been taught." Today's version of this lament would be "Their hearts aren't in it, and I won't stand for it!" These are the kinds of words that come only from someone who has been rejected by someone they care for. They are the opposite of indifference.

I struggled with this concept for the first few years of my walk with Jesus. My spiritual life was plain stressful because I couldn't grasp the fact that He was already and forever pleased to dwell with me. Although my mind accepted grace and forgiveness, my emotions weren't yet discipled into this truth. Every misstep and unrighteous thought felt like a good enough reason for God to withhold His blessings from me. Call it a religious misconception, faithlessness, or just emotional wounds, but it kept me from interacting with God in childlike trust. The funny thing about joining a church, however, is that even though your heart feels far from God, your body keeps doing what it feels like it should do. I found myself constantly going on mission trips, serving the church as a leader, and even preaching the Word of God! Yet my heart remained a stranger to His Presence because I couldn't communicate with a God that I thought was likely to be disappointed in me. This was until I found myself on a mission trip that required us to take medical services and supplies to a remote village deep in the mountains. Upon our arrival, the missionary team and the locals gathered for a worship service. Talk about an outpouring of the Holy Spirit! The place was alive with dancing and praise. Physical ailments were healed. Songs were sung with tears. It was a beautiful sort of chaos as I watched from the sidelines. I felt nothing. Actually, I felt less than nothing. I felt dead inside.

It's easy to blame the feeling of distance from God on your own lack and inability. You start to think things like, *Maybe I just have a hard time focusing* or *Maybe it's something I've done.* However, if I did anything right that evening, it was this. I interrupted my own self-pity session and went to a remote corner in the sanctuary. There, I got down on my knees and prayed the most honest prayer I knew how: "Jesus, I can't be who You want me to be. I don't think I ever could. But I love You. I hope that is enough." I didn't do anything fancy, nor did I follow a formula. I simply gave my authentic self to Him. And He received me with grace. Not even a minute later, I felt something blanket me, but it wasn't a physical blanket. Although I was in a sanctuary filled with people praying aloud and dancing to music, it felt like there were only two in the room—the Holy Spirit and me. And I felt a voice that, although not audible, was clear and weighty with peace.

"Faith, I love you anyway."

This was the revelation that breathed life into the theology I thought I knew. It was a revelation of His Presence. He showed me that He doesn't remain with me unconditionally just because He is good; He remains with me because He wants to! Even if you are having a poor mental health day, He is with you and loves you anyway. Even if you made a mistake at church, He is with you and loves you anyway. Even if you just yelled at your children in the car, He is with you and loves you anyway. This gives grace to the slow learner who needs time to grow according to His Word. This gives grace to the sensitive one who gets hurt deeply and can't forgive as quickly as others. This gives mercy to the wounded one who has been disappointed and put down and has become so jaded that the good news just doesn't hit home as easily.

Knowing that He delighted to dwell with me made our

connection so dear to me that it changed the way I lived. It changed how I woke up each day. I was more mindful of Him, more considerate. I was no longer in a rush to get up and go in the morning, but I began to greet the Holy Spirit, who had been watching over me at night. It changed how I made choices, for the Holy Spirit was available to offer wisdom and guidance. It even changed how I watched shows and movies! There were certain scenes that I just couldn't bear to sit through because I knew they were grievous to His Presence. It changed everything.

Daily Rhythms

A lifestyle that is centered on the Presence of God nurtures rhythms that draw us to Him. There is no one-size-fits-all formula to a Presence-centered life, because everyone's days have different demands. Nevertheless, the following are examples of everyday habits that take the tools of accessing His Presence and ingrain them in our lifestyle.

Rhythms of Gratitude

First Thessalonians 5:16–18 says, "Rejoice always, pray continually, give thanks in all circumstances; for this is God's will for you in Christ Jesus."

Rhythms of gratitude involve a habitual choice to recognize His Presence in every aspect of your life. You may know in your mind that God has been good to you, but when you sit in that reality with continual expressions of thanksgiving, you allow the rest of your being to connect to this truth. Giving Him thanks for the good weather or a productive day isn't just an obligation to check off your spiritual to-do list. Rather, it helps you feel what you already know—that a loving God is with you. Rhythms of praising Him can include a nightly gratitude journal, a habit of thanking Him for something every hour, or even just a shout of praise at random times of the day! Gratitude is not just an event to attend on occasion. Instead, it is like seasoning that you can sprinkle onto every aspect of your life.

Rhythms of Consultation

James 1:5 says, "If any of you lacks wisdom, you should ask God, who gives generously to all without finding fault, and it will be given to you."

Ask for guidance and wisdom often. Make it an instinct to look to Him whenever you are stuck or facing a challenge. Instead of defaulting to worrying or listening to other people's advice, you can make it a habit to consult Him first. Although social media influencers and your church pastors may know much, God knows more. You can interact with Jesus whenever you need help.

For every situation, He has wisdom from heaven that is available to you. Rhythms of consultation can look like praying before making a decision, taking a pause before reacting to bad news, or asking for help before entering a work meeting. By consulting Him step by step, you will receive His guidance at every turn. It won't always be an obvious response that shakes you into clarity. However, the nudge or the word that you receive from Him will be what you need in that moment. And then He will be available for the next moment.

If you are attempting to do this for the first time in your life, it is also helpful to surround yourself with God-fearing, biblically equipped followers of Jesus who will be able to help you discern whether you are hearing from God correctly. Over time, you will recognize how irreplaceable and life-giving the guidance of God is.

Rhythms of Grief

Psalm 34:18 says, "The LORD is close to the brokenhearted and saves those who are crushed in spirit."

Pain is to be expected in life, no matter how well behaved you have been or how well you can manage your circumstances. As letdowns come our way, we must regularly bring our sorrows to Jesus. Pain makes us deeply dissatisfied with empty religion. It causes us to reject shallow clichés and powerless traditions because we want nothing less than the pure, wise, and deep Presence of God. Presence is the only acceptable answer to deep pain. You must develop the habit of grieving with God, who guarantees His Presence to you in times of trouble.

You can have a journal for it or a go-to place to take a stroll. Every night, I like to do a "spiritual flush." I lie in bed and search my heart for any sorrow or burden that needs to be flushed out. Every offense and hurt must come out as an honest confession before God. They can come out with words, sighs, or tears. He has already seen these things in my heart, but the act of bringing them before Him connects me to Him in a deep way.

Rhythms of Petitioning

James 4:2 says, "You desire but do not have, so you kill. You covet but you cannot get what you want, so you quarrel and fight. You do not have because you do not ask God."

There are blessings God gives because of His grace, and

there are blessings He gives when we ask. We petition when we are confident in His ability to meet our needs. I used to have a Bible study with church members in my living room, and in the middle of it, one of my children would come in to ask me for a snack. You must really trust in your parent's love and believe in the power of your parent's permission to be so bold as to walk right into a group of adults and loudly ask for a cookie. Thankfully, there is no scheduled Bible study in heaven that makes it a bad time for us to approach our Father boldly like a child. I wonder how different the wilderness journey would have been for the Israelites if they had known how to trust in the power of petitioning God!

Regularly making requests to God about your needs and concerns is healthy for your soul. Nowhere does the Bible ever mention that a matter was too small to petition God for help. There is no requirement other than to genuinely approach His Presence to present your petition. So, ask often. Close your eyes to ask at the bus stop, or lift them in prayer while still in bed in the morning. Rhythms of petitioning aren't a magical formula that will suddenly grant you your every wish. However, they will enrich your days with a deep awareness of His kind and generous hand. You will intimately know Jehovah-jireh, the Lord who will provide.

The Power of a Holy Pause

The key to getting better at practicing the Presence of God is to do it often. Intimacy needs exercise, and the rhythms mentioned above are the soul's exercise equipment. Unfortunately, the demands in your life will always try to compete with this intention. However, when you fall out of intimacy with His

Presence, you can simply hop back in with a holy pause. A holy pause is literally just that—a pause. It isn't to be confused with passivity. Instead, it is an aggressive confrontation of anything and anyone that demands your obsessive attention. When you are in a whirlwind of emotions and distraction, *pause.* Breathe deeply and acknowledge Him. Turn your attention to Him for a moment. Allow the pressure you feel to bow to His peace. You can use this time to ask Him for help or simply to thank Him for being with you. This holy pause is a means to get back into step with God. It is the emergency brake when your vehicle is slipping. It is a way to ensure that you are making no decisions from fleshly compulsion but that you are remaining in Him. Holy pauses help keep your days Presence-centered.

Dear Friend of God

Let's not succumb to the religious pressure that tempts us to believe that we must now start earning His favor with this transformed lifestyle. Don't be afraid of baby steps! If you feel pressure to change every aspect of your life overnight, know that developing a Presence-centered life will take daily practice and time. I can't tell you how many of my grand resolutions to better align my life with His Presence have failed within weeks! I have started many journals that I never quite completed. I have prematurely ended many fasts. I have even forgotten to acknowledge Him for stretches of time. I have failed to consult Him about several important decisions. My confession here isn't meant to imply that inconsistency and broken promises should be rewarded. Rather, it is meant to magnify His grace— that He is with me still! Guilt and shame are weak motivations to go back to the throne room of His Presence. It is His kindness that leads us to repentance. I thank Him for the grace that always gives us a chance to return to Him, no matter how long it has been or how low we have fallen.

Your friendship with God begins at salvation, and you have access to Him before you do anything to change your life. To experience the riches of this friendship, however, you must make God a higher priority than your ambitions, goals, or standards. You must intentionally share your life with Jesus. Daily rhythms of accessing Him cultivate this kind of Presence-centered life. Yet, if you ever lose touch with these rhythms, don't dwell long in frustration. Simply get back on the horse and keep going, for God isn't in the rhythms! He is with you.

PART 3

Living as a
Friend of God

CHAPTER 7

Transformed by His Presence

I have tasted a thrill in fellowship with God which has made anything discordant with God disgusting.

—FRANK LAUBACH

One of my favorite experiences during my youth-ministry days was witnessing the utter freedom in students who would find the courage to repent and receive God's forgiveness. However, I also recognized the shame on some of their faces when a week or month later, they would show up to church after backsliding into their old ways. Eventually, I would find them lingering in the church lobby or outside the building. Adults can be the same way. When we fail or can't change, shame can convince us that we are separated from Christ.

Transformation is the Holy Spirit's work, but sometimes the pursuit of Christ can be disheartening. Regret over past wrongdoings can quench our will to pray. Regret over impurity can keep us from wanting to step foot in a church. Enough failures can trick us into believing that we can't change, and jadedness can callous our hearts. Transformation doesn't come easy, even if we are wanting to please Jesus. We can wonder what the point is in going to God if we have broken yet another promise or failed to maintain another commitment.

The longing to be better isn't a bad thing, for even Jesus said, "Be perfect, therefore, as your heavenly Father is perfect."* However, the pursuit of growth can replace the pursuit of His Presence and eventually stunt growth itself. Overcoming bad habits, avoiding mistakes, and defeating unrighteous mindsets aren't the ultimate goals of Christianity. Nevertheless, we can become consumed with the "shoulds" and "shouldn'ts," to the point that we become worshippers of transformation more than of Christ Himself. The result is a powerless Christianity, a religion that simply doesn't work. Knowing Jesus and following Him are the ultimate goals, and transformation is a fruit of these goals. It is paramount that we make this distinction clear.

We can mistake behavior change and good works as the means to Him rather than the result of Him. We can spend our entire faith journey on self-discovery and self-improvement without ever really knowing what the Holy Spirit thinks or says. If our focus is just on becoming better people, then it is, at the end of the day, about us—a moralistic pursuit. We don't need a relationship with the Holy Spirit to pursue that goal. Thankfully, Jesus didn't come to earth, die on the cross, and rise again so that He could create an exclusive club of the well-behaved. Instead, He did it to make us His friends.

Where Transformation Begins

Transformation begins when we are with God. Certainly, biblical knowledge helps, and there is value in receiving wisdom

* Matthew 5:48.

from experienced teachers. However, there is a kind of change that can come only from sitting with Jesus. Whether you are encountering His love afresh, wrestling with your doubts, or remaining silent with hot tears of grief washing down your face, every moment with the Holy Spirit changes you.

Dwelling with the Presence of God has a visible, transformative effect. Moses had been with God, and it was obvious to those around him because his face shone! Exodus 34:29–30 says, "When Moses came down from Mount Sinai with the two tablets of the covenant law in his hands, he was not aware that his face was radiant because he had spoken with the LORD. When Aaron and all the Israelites saw Moses, his face was radiant, and they were afraid to come near him."

It was no secret that Moses was speaking with God and dwelling in His Presence, for the evidence was in his transformation. There is no implication in this passage that this was a figurative sort of radiance. He needed an actual veil to cover his face. The glory left a trace on his countenance, and it was proof that he had been with the Presence of God.

The transformation was not just external but internal as well. The glory also left a trace on Moses's soul, for he was endowed with strength and wisdom to do the impossible for decades. Would it have been remotely possible for Moses to carry the weight of leading the people through the wilderness if he hadn't intimately known God's Presence? Throughout their wandering, Israel was stubbornly rebellious. They not only distrusted Yahweh's words but also tested Moses's leadership time and time again.* Leading a people like this was no small feat, and their disobedience would have been enough to drive anyone to quit. Yet Moses, once a murderer, runaway, and insecure leader, became the leader Israel needed by regu-

* Psalm 106.

larly doing one thing—dwelling with the Presence in the tabernacle. While simply wandering with God for decades, he was able to shepherd a mass of oppressed Hebrew slaves as they became a victorious nation. No program, PowerPoint presentation, or guru could take credit for Moses's transformation. He didn't have VIP seats for a conference, nor did he have the perfect pastor that took him under his wing. No, he just consistently sat with Yahweh. Although you may not be Moses, you have access to God that he never had. His Presence was before Moses, but His Presence is within you. Never undervalue the significance of this miracle! The transformation that Moses experienced is but a shadow of what you are meant to experience, because His Presence is now within us. Second Corinthians 3:18 says, "We all, who with unveiled faces contemplate the Lord's glory, are being transformed into his image with ever-increasing glory, which comes from the Lord, who is the Spirit."

Have you ever been with someone who wears heavy perfume or cologne? You can sit by them for five minutes and end up smelling like them for the rest of the day! Such is the effect of dwelling with the Holy Spirit. Abide in His Presence, and allow His glory to leave a trace on your life. Spend the day smelling like Jesus! Peter and John sure did when they faced the threats and judgment of the religious leaders of their day. The rulers, elders, and teachers ganged up on these preachers with intimidation and threats. However, in the face of it all, Peter and John remained committed to preaching the truth. And as we see in Acts 4:13, "When they saw the courage of Peter and John and realized that they were unschooled, ordinary men, they were astonished and they took note that *these men had been with Jesus.*" These previously unequipped, untrained, uncharismatic humans had been transformed because of their friendship with God! This change was not earned but rather given by the Holy Spirit.

The thing that Moses, Peter, and John had in common was that they had been with God. It wasn't something that just happened during Sunday gatherings or when it was most convenient. Moses chose to converse with God while under immense stress. It's easy to use stress as an excuse not to pray. Peter dove out of the boat to swim to Jesus, despite having renounced Him not long before. Guilt is often a reason we avoid God. John remained by Jesus's side as he saw Him bleeding on the cross, which challenged everything John ever had believed about Him. Disappointment is like a blunt blow to our devotion, but John chose to stay regardless. Yes, they had been with God. Their deliberate choice to remain through these tensions changed them forever.

When you have been with God, you have a personal history with Him. This history of fighting battles side by side and enduring waiting seasons together transforms us, just like our deepest friendships. Our closest friends don't earn seats in our innermost circle just because they were present for our mountaintop moments. No, the ones we bare our souls to and trust the most have walked with us in the ugliness, hardship, and humiliation of the valleys.

Change isn't always overt and immediate. You won't always sense it as it's happening. Even when there is nothing but silence, something deep is happening within you. Circumstances may not be changing to your liking, but you are most definitely changing to His likeness. An authentic relationship with the Holy Spirit is what alters the heart, sanctifies the mind, and brings out all that is good from within you. Galatians 5:16 says, "So I say, walk by the Spirit, and you will not gratify the desires of the flesh." How do you overcome temptations and become more like Jesus? Through the empowerment of the Spirit that comes from remaining with Him.

Come Alive in His Presence

My husband can always tell when I have been spending time with Jesus. As I'm someone who is prone to grumpy, moody mornings, he is excited when he finds me buried in my Bible, lingering over my piano, or interceding aloud in the bedroom at the start of the day. He says it's because when I do, I come alive. I have extra pep in my step as I wake up my four children for school. I'm singing in the hallways and not frustrated when breakfast isn't eaten quickly even though the school bus is about to arrive. Somehow I have patience when things go missing and the dogs endlessly bark. I'm steady when disappointment comes my way. My soul isn't running on fumes when I take time to dwell with my Heavenly Friend.

This is because God's Presence is the source of life! When you hang out in His courts, you encounter a vitality that can be found nowhere else.

Psalm 84:4–7 says,

Blessed are those who dwell in your house;
    they are ever praising you.

Blessed are those whose strength is in you,
    whose hearts are set on pilgrimage.
As they pass through the Valley of Baka,
    they make it a place of springs;
    the autumn rains also cover it with pools.
They go from strength to strength,
    till each appears before God in Zion.

This psalm was written by the Korahites, the sons of Korah who dedicated their lives to serving in the temple of God. Their calling was to oversee the dwelling place of His Presence, and they wrote this not just as a song but also as a testimony. They witnessed the transformative blessing experienced by those whose hearts were set on the journey to be with God. According to the psalmists, the ones who dwell with Him will be so content that they will overflow with praise. Those who seek Him for strength will indeed find it. Those who live to be with God will see their Valley of Baka turn into a place of springs. *Baka* means "weeping." Those in pursuit of Him can have their sorrows redeemed and receive life overflowing! Not only does His Presence transform us, but the journey of befriending His Presence transforms us as well. We come alive in the process.

The world likes to dish out formulas on how to live the blessed life. From a young age, we are asked, "What will you be when you grow up?" sparking dreams of what we could gain if we set our minds to it. And later, as we enter college and begin our careers, we are made to believe that a certain vocation, status, or asset will be the key to truly living. When we scroll on our phones, we look at these picture-perfect smiles, and it feels as if those people have it all together! Isn't that why we follow that influencer or subscribe to that YouTube channel? Often it is because we believe that they have the tools and inspiration we need. Whether it be health, wealth, or relational goals, society teaches us to obsess over these supposed keys to the blessed life, while forgetting the only One who has the power to bless. The strength and gladness for living come from the Holy Spirit. I have had the honor of sitting with dreamers with shattered hopes, parents who had to bury a child, ex-congregants who went through a painful exit from church, and so on. Their realities were so crushing that only the Presence of God was able to sustain them. When even the best of friends can't understand, Jesus can. When even the most revelatory books and podcasts can't guide, God can. For those whose souls need emergency CPR, the Presence of God is the life force that resuscitates. With Him, we come alive.

Love and Obedience

Loving God enables us to obey Him. Love is self-sacrificing affection and commitment. We sacrifice for what we love. We put in time and hard work to achieve success. We invest much planning and money in raising our children. Even painful procedures and body-tearing workouts reveal our commitment to our health or physical appeal. Love is a force of devotion that lifts something or someone over oneself. This is what Jesus did for us, which is why Scripture says that God is love.* In turn, our love for Yahweh empowers us to place Him first and obey.

The other day I caught sight of something at home that triggered a memory of a time when I felt deeply wronged by someone. Don't you hate it when little things can trigger you just like that? As I was casually doing chores around the house, I came across some old papers and was immediately immersed in painful memories of having trusted someone who ultimately took advantage of my ministry and my family. I stood in the middle of the room, unable to move because I was barraged with angry thoughts about what I should have said and what this person really deserved. After a few minutes of this torment, I reached for His Presence. I whispered, "Jesus . . ." That's all it took to grab hold of Him. From there, I began speaking my thoughts in the most honest way I knew how. I

* 1 John 4:16.

told Him that I knew all the Bible verses about forgiveness and turning the other cheek but that it still felt deeply unjust. After I poured out the last drops of my bitterness at His feet, I felt His gentle voice say, "What if I asked you to forgive, not because it's fair but because you would become more like Me?" As I stood there, I wrestled with this. Was becoming like Jesus enough for me? What happened next can't be explained by anything other than the committed love that exists between two friends. I ultimately sighed out a "yes" not because I am an exceptional person. It wasn't because the person I needed to forgive deserved it either. Simply put, it was only because my dear Jesus asked me to forgive. Although, from a human perspective, I had every right to remain bitter and offended, my love for Him mysteriously and supernaturally made obedience worth it.

When obedience is difficult, try focusing on falling in love with His Presence. When you grow in closeness to someone, you become aware of what is important to them, and you are willing to prioritize it. Our affection for Him compels us to care about what He cares about, even if it causes inconvenience or requires us to sacrifice worldly pleasure. The more you intentionally seek His will and follow it, the more you realize that the reward of obedience is a deeper enjoyment of His Presence. In every moment, what matters to God? What does He want from you and for you while you are interacting with your co-workers? What is important to Him as you clean your room? Seeking His will and obeying it keeps you immersed in Him. An intimate, authentic, and passionate friendship with Jesus infuses you with the grace you need to surrender your agenda and live by His ways.

Friendship over Perfectionism

Love, joy, peace, patience, kindness, generosity, faithfulness, gentleness, and self-control are all attributes we strive for. Yet so often, we try to conjure these up through our own goodwill and self-discipline. We create resolutions. We log our progress in journals. We try to muster up strength from the depths of our being. Yet according to Galatians 5:22–23, it is the Holy Spirit's work to create this fruit, while it is our work to walk step by step with Him. If we try to transform without practicing the Presence of God, we draw on our limited reservoir of energy and understanding. This often leads to self-condemnation and striving.

Befriending the Holy Spirit isn't just about having a regimented devotional life. He is a divine companion and not a duty. Sometimes our relationship with God can become coldly transactional. You may intentionally be refraining from sin because you know you have a big project coming up and you need His support. You may find yourself attending an extra prayer meeting in the hope of appeasing a God who is supposedly disappointed by your poor behavior that week. You may open the Bible because you don't feel righteous. When we conduct our spiritual lives this way, we play the earning game with Jesus. We try to use our devotion to get Him to approve and bless where we need it.

True spiritual transformation begins with authentic friendship. It's not about becoming or achieving. It's about being with Him. This comes first. As the friendship gets richer, you start to understand His heart. You know what grieves Him and quenches Him. You see things from His point of view. Being on the same page with Jesus inspires us to want to stay on the same page. Our desire to change is no longer the fruit of obligation or shame but rather the fruit of love.

Galatians 5:25 says, "Since we live by the Spirit, let us keep in step with the Spirit."

You don't have to strive for perfection. Instead, you can focus on stewarding this very moment with God. And after this moment passes, you can focus on the next. As you make every decision, you heed His counsel. During every loss, you mourn with the ever-present Helper. When you fail, you repent and trust the Advocate. Every moment is an opportunity for an interaction of some sort because He is available, accessible, and kind. You don't have to consider everything you must do; rather, focus on what He is leading you to do *right now.* Even when a task feels impossible to accomplish, breathe and petition Him for supernatural strength. The accumulation of these moments produces the fruit of the Spirit! As you take it moment by moment and step by step, He will build your character and shape your heart.

When Stuck

I have come across countless incredible people who lamented their inability to live up to biblical standards. Secret sins, dark comforts, and warped thought patterns are no strangers to Christians. Someone once approached me in tears over his inability to overcome a debauched lifestyle. He wept in confession, and soon he rolled his eyes while saying, "So, do I just read the Bible or something?" The message was loud and clear—he didn't think God could change him. While he was drowning in the mire of his thoughts, the whole "God is with you" speech wouldn't have been helpful, because he was, as we all are at times, stuck. Even if you had paid for his registration for the most anointed Christian conference, he wouldn't have had the will to attend. Even if you had made a daily devotional booklet just for him, keeping up with it would have been an impossible challenge. There are countless stories like this in the church. The single parent who is too tired to praise. The person who is struggling with mental health to the point where it's a miracle if they can even get out of bed. How is practicing the Presence of God possible when you are too stuck to change? The following tools can help you wiggle your way out. Even if you manage to use only one, it is a step forward, and each step is worth celebrating.

1. Ask Him for Help

Just ask. When you are smothered in a pile of your own mistakes, call out for mercy. Ask Him to do what you can't do. This isn't a cop-out. It isn't excusing yourself from trying to do the right thing. Rather, it is humility. You honor Him when you recognize that only He is able to help you. Ask Him to create in you what you can't conjure up on your own.

Psalm 51:10 says, "Create in me a pure heart, O God, and renew a steadfast spirit within me."

2. Ask Him to Reveal Lies

The cause of dysfunction can be deep-rooted lies. These deceptions could stem from your childhood, from trauma, or from the influence of others. You might believe that you have no hope or that your life doesn't matter. Ask God to show you the lie and to replace it with His truth!

Psalm 139:23–24 says, "Search me, God, and know my heart; test me and know my anxious thoughts. See if there is any offensive way in me, and lead me in the way everlasting."

3. Reject Hindrances

If you can pinpoint a hindrance to your sanctification, reject it. Anything that keeps you from living by truth doesn't belong in your life. You will know it by what it produces in you. Does it nurture a deeper closeness with Jesus, or does it harden your heart even further? It could be a television show, an application on your phone, or an unhealthy lifestyle. Throw it off!

Hebrews 12:1–2 says, "Let us throw off everything that hinders and the sin that so easily entangles. And let us run with perseverance the race marked out for us, fixing our eyes on Jesus, the pioneer and perfecter of faith."

4. Invite the Friends of God

Invite others to join you in the fight to believe. If you don't have faith yourself, welcome others who do. Text them and ask for prayer. Having one or two people praying on your behalf makes a difference. Find a fellow believer who can join you in Bible reading or attend church services with you. Sometimes it is the faith of our friends that carries us to Jesus, just as the men in Mark 2 carried their paralyzed friend.

Verses 3–5 say,

Some men came, bringing to him a paralyzed man, carried by four of them. Since they could not get him to Jesus because of the crowd, they made an opening in the roof above Jesus by digging through it and then lowered the mat the man was lying on. When Jesus saw their faith, he said to the paralyzed man, "Son, your sins are forgiven."

Dear Friend of God

Perfection isn't a requirement for experiencing friendship with God. Maintaining your sober streak isn't a prerequisite to approaching Jesus. Having fallen into sexual sin doesn't prevent you from being able to call Him friend. The Cross guarantees you the freedom to speak to Him after you hurt someone, break a promise, or fail to keep your thoughts clean. Transformation isn't a precondition for accessing the Presence of God, but accessing the Presence of God will result in transformation. If experiencing friendship with God becomes your life's pursuit, you won't remain the same.

So, don't wait. Don't wait until you have your life together to speak to Him. Don't wait until you feel holy to sit with Him. You don't have to shake off a sense of guilt before you pray. Pray first, and allow the Holy Spirit to address your burdens. He will accept you as you are, and He will also sanctify you. He can do both. When our relationship with Jesus blossoms, so does a love that inspires us and empowers us to become more like our dear Friend.

CHAPTER 8

Propelled by His Presence

The union of the Holy Spirit with the human will give birth to charity.

—BERNARD OF CLAIRVAUX, *The Steps of Humility and Pride*

What if the most world-changing and history-making thing you can do is to befriend the Presence of God? Some of the most profound moments in biblical history were propelled by those who were in intimate relationship with His Presence—David defeating Goliath, Daniel surviving the lion's den, Esther saving her people, Peter walking on water, and so many others. The impact they made wasn't due to their popularity, capability, or remarkability. Instead, it was the result of making space for His voice and following His lead. We live in a time when the hustle and grind are glorified. But what if you can change the world with your friendship with Jesus? The Presence of God and our mission on earth are intertwined.

Befriending Jesus doesn't culminate with your enlightenment and betterment. Rather, it becomes the foundation for serving and blessing others. The Holy Spirit isn't stagnant. Although He dwells with you, friendship with Him propels you to reach other places and people. The things that happen in our secret place with Him will overflow into the public space because anyone who carries God's Presence is also carrying a kingdom movement. He loves to sit with you, but He also wants to move through you to invite others into friendship.

Some of the greatest spiritual awakenings and revival movements have occurred as a result of people communing with His Presence. The Great Pyongyang Revival of 1907 was an evangelistic movement that gave this city in northern Korea the nickname "the Jerusalem of the East" during a time of political instability, poverty, and pain from colonial oppression. No preacher was the face of this movement. No impressive amounts of money were poured into the mission work at this time. On the contrary, six months before this spiritual awakening began, Korean Christians and Western missionaries held prayer meetings each day. A Korean Christian even held one at his church every morning at 5 A.M., encouraging the hungry and broken to wake up to be with God before doing anything else. After those six months, a revival broke out among a weary people, and a mass movement of conversions and inner healing began to spread throughout the nation. People who had nothing found their everything in His Presence.

Being a companion of the Holy Spirit isn't just a personal choice; it is also a missional one that has an impact on others. William Seymour was a one-eyed son of formerly enslaved African Americans. He led a spiritual awakening known as the Azusa Street Revival in 1906 in Los Angeles. Seymour was so marginalized that he had to attend seminary classes while sitting in the hallway outside the classroom, and even his own church rejected him and locked him out of the building. He had nothing but Jesus. He started prayer meetings in a house for those willing to join. From there, a revival broke out that was so prolific it gained global attention and fueled the spread of the modern-day Pentecostal movement. Seymour had no status or clout to create this by his own means. God does incredible things with those who abide in His Presence. Seymour was simply a friend of God who walked with Him in the wilderness season of his life.

The Impact of the Wilderness: Rahab's Testimony

The wilderness can make us feel useless and disqualified from participating in God's mission. Waiting for breakthroughs can feel like wasted time. The wandering doesn't seem to serve a purpose other than to open our eyes to the harsh realities of life. Especially within cultures where accomplishments are adulated and progress is commended, fruitlessness and standstills are usually disdained. Yet God's Presence makes the wilderness matter. If our friendship with God is what allows us to be a blessing to others, then we can make a positive impact even while in the wilderness. Wanderers in the wasteland can still be used by God because kingdom impact is determined by who you are with.

To the Israelites, walking the endless terrain may have felt like the tough consequence of their disobedience, but the world got to witness a chosen people walking hand in hand with their God for decades. Their plans were uncertain, but to onlookers, what God was doing was clear. Not only does God exist, but He also sticks with His people and protects them. Battles were won and sustenance was provided, and the only explanation was that Yahweh was with them. Israel may have felt like they were wasting time, but their wandering was also testifying about the one true God to every passerby and every village along the way. Kingdom impact isn't determined by our ability to get to our coveted destination. It also isn't attained by our record of perfect choices. Rather, kingdom impact is God's work, and we partake in it by remaining with Him. We see this from Rahab's testimony:

> I know that the LORD has given you this land and that a great fear of you has fallen on us, so that all who live in this country are melting in fear because of you. We have heard how the LORD dried up the water of the Red Sea for you when you came out of Egypt, and what you did to Sihon and Og, the two kings of the Amorites east of the Jordan, whom you completely destroyed. When we heard of it, our hearts melted in fear and everyone's courage failed because of you, for the LORD your God is God in heaven above and on the earth below.*

Her confession was poignant for the two Israelite spies she was surreptitiously hosting. It was at last time for God's people to leave the wilderness. Moses had passed away, and new leadership had stepped in—Joshua, the apprentice who had sat in Yahweh's Presence for decades. He secretly sent two men to scout the land, particularly Jericho. An alert went out to the king of Jericho at the first sight of these men, but little did he know that they were hidden in the house of a prostitute. When the king's men showed up, she risked her life to protect two strangers that weren't of her creed or her people. She went to great lengths to cover for these foreign intruders. However,

* Joshua 2:9–11.

once the authorities departed, she revealed her reason. It was faith.

Rahab came to know Yahweh through the Israelites' journey. She knew God although she had never met Him. Rahab's testimony reveals what the Almighty can do with our lives when we adhere to Him in our most barren seasons. He is always doing something outside our realm of capability and influence. Friends of God can believe that God's goodness will triumph in ways that aren't attainable by our own strength. Faith isn't just a ticket out of the wilderness. It is the belief that God can move even when we aren't moving. God can use our lives even when they are in shambles. We don't have to reach a destination or be exceptional for the Holy Spirit to use us as a vessel of blessing. Kingdom impact is a by-product of friendship with God.

In the decades of waiting, the Lord was setting the stage for Israel's entrance into the Promised Land. Stories of Yahweh and His chosen people spread because God carried those stories, and eyewitness accounts became legends because His favor made it so. The world around them was sufficiently primed with God's message, and their wandering made history. Other nations grew in awareness of God, and some, like Rahab, began to have faith. The battle for Jericho and the new lands was already won before Israel even had a chance to pick up a sword. God knew what He was doing all along.

Don't be fooled by the apparent meaningless of your wilderness wandering, for God is still up to something! We see that throughout the Bible.

Hannah's wilderness was barrenness in her womb, but in answer to her cries, God blessed Israel with a prophet.

David's wilderness was running away from a king who hated him, but from it came songs that bless us still today.

Mary's wilderness was a virgin birth, but this service to God ultimately saved the world.

Kingdom impact is determined not by our might nor by favorable circumstances. None of these biblical heroes had the marks of greatness. They just remained with God in the wilderness, and through that, God used their lives to make an impact on others. Stick with His Presence. Purpose, provision, and redemption come after. Stick with Jesus, and in His good time, you will be where you are meant to be. Stick with His Presence more than your plans.

God can do more with your loyalty in the wilderness than you can by yourself in the Promised Land. Instead of earning your way to advancements and accomplishments, may you be propelled into them. As you wander through the wasteland of disappointment and closed doors, the temptation to go your own way is real. But if you keep following Jesus, you go where only He can take you. In the end, there are doors that only the Spirit can open. Only Christ can change hearts. To be propelled into our God-given destiny, we must abide in His Presence. It can feel as if His timing isn't quick enough and His plan isn't good enough. However, Rahab's testimony proves that, despite our track record of pitfalls and our history of regret, God can still do a great work with our lives. As John 15:5 says, "If you remain in me and I in you, you will bear much fruit; apart from me you can do nothing."

Plunder for the Next Season

The wilderness is a vulnerable journey that can take much away from you. While you are navigating this harsh terrain, following Jesus doesn't always feel victorious. It can feel backward and foolish, especially when you are . . .

- praising Him in a hospital room while the results don't look favorable
- trusting Him at the end of the month when finances run dry
- loving people that treat you unfairly
- serving Him when you see no positive results
- continuing to pray when there haven't been any visible answers

Yet God is faithful, even when the wilderness is merciless and our behavior in it is shameful. Before Moses passed away, he addressed Israel, chronicling their wilderness journey, beginning to end. His account is filled with all that God had done for Israel. Although it took forty years to move His people out of the wilderness, God was never not moving. The redeeming work continued, even when Israel disobeyed and wasn't where they wanted to be. Exodus 12:37 tells us that about six hundred thousand Israelite men left Egypt on foot, making the entire nation a mass of approximately two million, counting women and children. This was quite a crowd that would have needed to learn how to function as a unified nation and stewards of their own land. This molding and growing transpired in the wilderness. The forty years of wandering formed Israel. Throughout the years, they appointed leaders, developed a government, were introduced to God's character, and learned the importance of obedience to Yahweh. They received decrees and laws that not only kept them close to His Presence but protected them as well. They learned the pathways to blessings. They had unprecedented battle training with a God that fought with them and for them. They were a far cry from being abandoned to wither in the wilderness! This was their training ground and their spiritual school. At the end of it all, they didn't enter the Promised Land with nothing to their names. On the contrary, they left the wilderness with a plunder of growth and readiness.

You may feel like anything but a winner right now. Or you may look back on seasons past and find that the gain didn't outweigh the cost, that the lessons learned weren't worth the pain. You may not have been victorious in the battle for faith, and you may not have a testimony to share—yet. To have blazing faith in this moment is to believe that He is doing something in the unseen and unfelt and that it is for your good. This belief doesn't have to be confirmed by a surge of emotion. It just needs to be acknowledged and given a chance. This isn't to blanket your sorrows with Christian jargon, implying that God stole your happy days to make you stronger or give you something better. Rather, it is to say that your barrenness won't have the final word. Nothing is wasted as you remain in His Presence. And when seasons change, you will move forward with the plunder that you gained from the wilderness.

Moving with God

"I'm a Creaster!"

The first time I heard someone say this, I was bewildered. What this person meant was that she worshipped Jesus on Christmas and Easter. She was willing to sacrifice the time to be with God on those days, but any other day was hers to control. She was willing to meet with God at those times but not to be led by Him at any other time. Her holidays were His, but her life was her own. There is no question that these gatherings and moments are significant, but if the Spirit wants to do more, are we available and accessible to Him? We've talked about how

He is with you wherever you go. The question now is, Are you willing to go wherever He wants to take you? We tend to limit how God can bless us and use us because we don't follow His leading. We offer ourselves in our moment of prayer, but we take ourselves back after prayer time has finished. Those who know His Presence must also know how to follow Him in the work He is doing. If He called you to another land or even across the street, would you move with Him? If He asked you to extend a humble hand of help to someone, would you allow your schedule to be interrupted?

Having had four children, each less than two years apart, means that I had the privilege and challenge of raising quite a few toddlers in my earlier years of motherhood. I can assure you that just because someone loves you and is dependent on you doesn't mean that they know how to follow your lead. I have had one too many incidents in grocery stores, stuck in the baking aisle, with children pulling the cart in different directions. Out come the coaxing and compromise, and everything takes much longer than it should. Now that my children are a bit more mature, going places and doing things together is much easier. Now when I say "This way," they follow. At the words "Wait here," they remain. Our ability to do activities together is greater. Our mutual trust is also deeper. We can go to far more places and get many more things accomplished simply because they have matured enough to follow my lead. The same goes for our faith. Spiritual immaturity leaves us unwilling to follow God, like a toddler in aisle 16. Yet He has people He would like us to meet and places He would like to take us. This is because our friendship with God is missional.

You know that you are moving with God's Presence when . . .

- you seek His will and wish to follow it
- you recognize opportunities to serve others
- you are willing to be inconvenienced or interrupted by His will
- you are compelled by love for others
- you are able to part ways with ego and pride

It is important to note that the story of the two spies and Rahab wasn't Israel's first go at scouting the Promised Land. God tried to lead His people into the Promised Land decades prior. Yet they refused to be led! This scene of rebellion is recounted in Numbers 14. From Egypt through the wilderness, God had displayed great loyalty to Israel, despite their incessant grumbling. But Israel's loyalty was limited by their fear, pride, and compulsions. Despite the report that the land was good for the taking, all Israel could see was the prospect of failure and destruction. They refused to believe Him. Their fear diminished Him. Their pride ignored Him. Their compulsions elevated their agenda over Him. Despite having seen the plagues and heard His laws and precepts, Israel refused to move with Yahweh into the land of their destiny. They chose wandering over moving with God's Presence. What does it take to move with Him? Faith. A lot of things can draw you to sit with Jesus—the need for comfort, a desperation for help, or a longing for meaning. However, it takes faith to move with Jesus. Hebrews 11:1 says that faith is "assurance about what we do not see." Faith is basically trusting God enough to give Him a chance. Faith would have moved with Yahweh out of the wilderness and into the Promised Land.

The Presence-Centered Mission

The Presence-centered life isn't an idle life. It doesn't peak when you are satisfied with your Bible studies and morning devotionals. Instead, it propels you to live out His mission on earth. When Isaiah encountered the heavenly splendor of the King in His throne room, he cried out, "Here am I. Send me!"* When Peter was restored by Jesus, he was told, "Feed my sheep."† Our intimacy with God takes us to places where others need the knowledge of His Presence. Those who sit with Him will also be sent by Him.

If you don't love or even take an interest in your neighbor of different faith, then your Christianity may have become more about your own growth than about Jesus Himself. Institutions, programs, and people that have contorted Christian living into a self-help agenda are void of intimacy with Jesus because an honest relationship with the Holy Spirit will transform our hearts to beat like His. He is love, and knowing Him causes us to love others. As 1 John 4:19–20 reminds us, "We love because he first loved us. Whoever claims to love God yet hates a brother or sister is a liar. For whoever does not love their brother and sister, whom they have seen, cannot love God, whom they have not seen."

If the Christian lifestyle that we cultivate isn't Presence-centered, it will become self-centered. The mission of a self-centered Christian is to build a good life on earth. However, Jesus offers us a better dream. The mission of a Presence-centered Christian is to enjoy God while bringing others into the friendship as well. What makes being on mission for Jesus

* Isaiah 6:8.
† John 21:17.

special isn't the grandeur of the call. Neither is it the significance of the work. The most valuable thing about being on mission for Jesus is that He guarantees His Presence as we allow ourselves to be sent in His name. The point of making disciples of all nations and loving our neighbor is to do it with Him.

When Yahweh sent Moses to free His people, the only certainty He provided was "I will be with you."* When Joshua was commissioned to break a forty-year streak of wandering and lead Israel into the Promised Land, he was given the same promise: "I will be with you."† Jesus echoed this assurance after giving His disciples the mission to reach the rest of the world with the good news: "Surely I am with you always, to the very end of the age."‡

There is a pattern here. Friends of God get placed on holy assignment to do things that are beyond their capacity. These things are often awkward, inconvenient, or downright impossible. After the assignment is given, God offers us the gift of Himself. He doesn't spend time hyping us up, praising our abilities, or coddling our insecurities. Instead, He simply guarantees His friendship. This friendship empowers us for the assignment. He is the means. He is the reason.

Jesus would love to use your beautiful life to bless your street, your community, even the world. Practicing the Presence isn't a mere exercise of piety. It releases God's redemptive power to others. Coffee with Jesus in the morning can translate to encouraging a co-worker during your fifteen-minute break. Meditating on His Word can create in you the compassion to sacrifice your time and money for someone in need. He has a mission on this earth to gather His children that they

* Exodus 3:12.
† Joshua 1:5.
‡ Matthew 28:20.

may know Him, and you are called to partner with Him in that mission.

Beyond the Wilderness

There have been a handful of moments when I wanted to forfeit my calling as a pastor and preacher of the gospel. This calling was near and dear to my heart because my Heavenly Father gave it to me at the age of seventeen. I began pastoring at nineteen, and it has been a thrill ride since. My service has always been my love letter to Him. The highs and lows didn't matter to me, because my joy was doing it with Him. However, as life usually goes, changes came my way. In my mid-twenties, I became a wife, then a mother. Then by thirty, I was a mother of four. The terrain of my life drastically altered within a few years. I used to travel around the world, and now all the traveling I was doing was to the nursery and the kitchen. I used to go to conferences and retreats, but now the main event was the one that started with cries at 3 A.M. After my fourth child, I was, inevitably, tired. It wasn't just physical fatigue. It was spiritual as well.

Trying to serve Jesus in spite of all my limitations as a young female pastor, pastor's wife, woman of color, and mother of young children eventually wore me out. I was tired of dreaming. I was tired of believing in more. I was tired of making plans that wouldn't work out. I was tired of investing in people who would walk away. My faith had lost its imagination, and my prayers were for survival.

This was my wilderness, and my companions for the journey were jadedness and hopelessness. However, before I threw in the towel once and for all, my husband counseled me to turn to the Presence. I entered a season of fasting and prayer. For almost six months, I opened the sanctuary of our church with no agenda other than to be with Him. There were some weeks when I would grieve for hours. There were other weeks when I would just sit still and feel nothing. The point wasn't to attain a feeling. It was just to be with Him.

After that six-month period, I woke up one morning with His voice ringing in my heart. He wanted me to start a women's conference. I was hesitant. I wasn't sure if there was even a need for one, since so many amazing women's ministries already existed. I had many reasons to say no. But all my time surrendering to Him gave me the inexplicable faith to say yes. I knew that voice because I had spent months listening to it. I got up and followed it, along with a few other women that I brought along for the venture. Over the next few months, we put together a modest women's conference at a local church, and it ended up drawing Asian American women from all over the United States. I will never forget the healing, connection, and revival I witnessed at that conference. Jesus was in it, and He resurrected the hope of the women in attendance. It was a movement birthed in His Presence. He prepared me for it in the wilderness, and He propelled me into it with His voice.

No wilderness is forever—only God is. Every difficulty and pain that is weighing you down will be outlasted by His Presence. And alongside Him, you will go through the desert and walk out of it with the experience, strength, and wisdom you need for the next season. I assure you again, no wilderness is forever—only God is. Let's hold on to forever.

Dear Friend of God

Your friendship with Jesus can change the world. Redemptive history wasn't shaped by the popular and successful. To serve

God and make an eternal impact, you don't need a higher education or a respectable reputation. If you scour the Bible, you will discover a slew of kingdom workers and world changers who simply sat with God and sought His will.

David wrote songs to Him in the wilderness.

Mary of Bethany poured perfume on Jesus's feet.

The apostles and other believers experienced an outpouring of the Holy Spirit in the upper room.

And so on.

The wilderness may be vast, but it can't contain Him. He will move in you and through you. Experiencing friendship with Jesus will also create in you a love for God's will. Brother Lawrence once said, "I'm not anxious about my purpose in life because I only want to do God's will."* Funny how the will of God for him was to enjoy His Presence in his simple—and dare I say mundane—days as a monk. And yet that precious and private relationship has echoed throughout history and blesses me—and now you—hundreds of years later. As you daily access His Presence, it may lead you to people or places that become your mission field. However, what's important here isn't the mission itself. Rather, it is the gift of moving with God.

Your days in the wilderness matter. You may be stuck in a rut, and your praises may be but a whisper, but nothing can dim His resurrection power, which remains with you. Today all you may be able to do is silently acknowledge Him while eating breakfast or taking that short walk to the mailbox. Thank God that the impact of our lives is determined by Jesus and not ourselves. Just as God used Israel's wandering to demonstrate His power to the nations around them, He can use you whether you are struggling or thriving.

* Brother Lawrence, *The Practice of the Presence of God* (New Kensington, Pa.: Whitaker House, 1982), 40.

What I wanted was simply to belong totally to God, so I decided to give everything I could give in order to attain the greatest blessing in return—knowing Him.

—BROTHER LAWRENCE, *The Practice of the Presence of God*

Your soul may feel lost in the wilderness, but take heart, for it is also where His Presence can be found. When I was looking for God as a child, I stumbled upon His name while sitting in a hotel room during family vacation, watching a gospel movie on the television. Before that, I had no idea that His name was Jesus! Even though I didn't know the gospel yet, that name felt dear to me. It felt like I had figured out a secret and discovered a key.

Years later, encountering Him and getting saved was not the culmination of my spiritual journey but rather just the start. Try flipping through the pages of the Bible, and you'll find that it is gushing with stories of human beings having a tangible relationship with God! I wanted that. I heard countless testimonies, but I wanted my own. When I listened to sermons, I was inspired to seek Him, but I wasn't sure how. When I went on mission trips, I witnessed His many works, and I was increasingly equipped to do more works for Him. When I read books, I attained incredible insight into the Christian faith. I knew more, thanks to these resources. When I sat under the tutelage of several anointed pastors, I received priceless wisdom. I have come to value all these things, but they weren't the object of my search. They didn't complete me. Neither did my achievements, the very achievements that I had ardently prayed over. Marriage and children were a gift, no doubt, but they weren't the object of my search either. When I accepted my calling to ministry and gave my whole life to preach the gospel, I was thrilled. But still, that wasn't the object of my search.

Ultimately, I found what I was looking for in the wilderness—that dry and barren wasteland of confusion, weakness, and sorrow. It was there that I befriended the Presence of God. In the years that I cried out to Him to free me from my wandering and waiting, I didn't know that He was answering an old prayer I had forgotten. It was the quiet prayer of a six-year-old Korean American girl who was looking for Jesus in the library. In the wilderness, He was fulfilling the desire of that little girl's heart. I used to disdain limitations, failures, and trials. I thought these things barred me from experiencing His Presence. Turns out that they became vehicles for a deeper intimacy. They ushered me right into the throne room and kept me there for years. The wilderness gave me a Friend.

It is human to despise the wilderness and its brutal terrain. No matter your religious affiliation or your record of good deeds, you will endure things on this earth that are beyond you. You will know shame that sticks to you like a scarlet letter. You will know worries that place the weight of the world on your shoulders. You will know rejection, and it will be completely unjust. You will know disappointment no matter how much you strategize your way through life. You will know closed doors that mercilessly remain sealed no matter how hard you kick and pound. You will know the anguish of waiting and utter helplessness. But as you endure this wilderness of the soul, know that you will find something else. A hope. A reward. A purpose. A companion. You will find His Presence.

Blessed Are You

So, blessed are you. Yes, you. Whether you are wandering in the desert or conquering the Promised Land, you are blessed as long as you are walking with Jesus. Despite the cruelty of the wilderness, you still have the power to make a choice. It is a choice that no amount of hardship or waiting can take away from you. It is the choice to befriend the Presence of God. On the journey, the blessing is the friendship, not the destination.

Deuteronomy 2:7 recounts, "The LORD your God has blessed you in all the work of your hands. He has watched over your journey through this vast wilderness. These forty years the LORD your God has been with you, and you have not lacked anything."

This verse is mind-bogglingly rich with grace. Didn't God Himself call Israel a stiff-necked people who were difficult to lead? They grumbled over meals. They rebelled out of fear. They opposed Moses, God's appointed leader. They even spoke against God Himself. And despite all the signs that God had given them, they turned to idolatry. These trespasses brought discipline and correction from God. But still, God remained, and as long as God remained with His people, they were blessed. This blessing wasn't just a positive emotion that confirmed God's love for them. No, this blessing was a manifestation of God's favor, seen in the work of their hands and in daily provision. To all the nations that were witnesses to Israel's journey, it was clear that these people were different. They were with God.

A deep knowledge of theology won't usher you out of the pit of pain and loss. However, a knowledge of His Presence can. Your favorite preacher won't sit with you in your most humiliating moments. But the Holy Spirit will. Your podcasts won't comfort you when you are misunderstood. But He will. He always will.

Hope in His Presence

You can know the Presence of God no matter what season you are in. You can befriend Him just as you are. It isn't a nirvanic state attained by the extra spiritual. It isn't for the super-Christians who have a special calling to hear His voice. It definitely isn't just for the ones who rarely sin or the ones who do a lot of good. The Presence of God has been made available for everyone who wants Him. Jesus made sure of it. This gives us great hope.

The Presence of God is good news for the ones who have failed. If you are in the wilderness because of great failure, you probably drink from the well of regret every day. You can't dream, because you feel as though you have no right. Crippling guilt anchors you to the past, and you endure its punishment because you dare not believe that you can move on. If you are still muddling through the wreckage of your mistakes, have hope. He is with you, and in Him is unending grace. You don't have to clean up the mess before you approach Him. He can be found now, and He has mercy for you.

The Presence of God is good news for the broken and disappointed. If your wilderness is an unending desert of bad news and tragedy, your faith may be tired and your heart empty of joy. Helplessness has become your norm, and you have decided to settle because the blow of another letdown is too much for you to bear. Your soul is parched. You have no more songs to sing and no more prayers to pray. Have hope. He is with you still. His friendship is an oasis. Allow His words to water your soul.

The Presence of God is good news for the marginalized. If you are in the wilderness because you are being unfairly treated or overlooked, know this—the Presence of God determines the impact of your life. He is the one who gives you your calling. The significance of your life isn't dependent on those with power and connections. The Presence of God will guide you to your destination, no matter what walls stand before you. He was able to take a young pregnant girl named Mary, with no riches or title to her name, and change the world through her yielded life. God loves to intertwine His glorious story with those who are unseen and unheard of.

Every need in life can be met by abiding in His Presence. If you need endurance, His company will comfort you. If you need to balance all of life's demands, His voice will lead you step by step. If you need guidance, He has wisdom for anyone who is willing to sit at His feet and remain. Abide in Him and follow His lead. He will take you through the wilderness and to your promised destination. As you experience this friendship with God, may you be able to echo the cry of the psalmist in Psalm 73:25–28 (MSG):

> You're all I want in heaven!
>   You're all I want on earth!
> When my skin sags and my bones get brittle,
>   GOD is rock-firm and faithful.

Look! Those who left you are falling apart!
   Deserters, they'll never be heard from again.
But I'm in the very presence of God—
   oh, how refreshing it is!
I've made Lord GOD my home.
   God, I'm telling the world what you do!

Everything you want and need is with you right now. No matter the mess your life is in or the state of your mental health, He is with you. The struggle to make your life matter was already won by Jesus. He won't be convinced by your hard work or your ability to manage. He is convinced by the Cross. You can rest from striving, and you can stop searching. Because He is "with you always, to the very end of the age."*

---

* Matthew 28:20.

AUTHOR'S NOTE

H is name used to be Nicholas Herman. Today we know him as Brother Lawrence. He became an author when his personal conversations and letters were published after his death. He didn't preach to crowds, and he didn't have followers and fans. He has no grand accomplishments to his name, nor did he build anything that has lasted to this day. He was simply a friend. Most notably, he was a friend of God.

Brother Lawrence wasn't always overflowing with the divine revelations that he is now known for. In fact, he struggled to grasp the fullness of God's grace for quite some time, and he went through a dark ten-year season of wrestling with shame and anxiety. The pivotal moment that propelled him out of this season was when he reached the end of himself. After ten years of wrestling with his faith, he ultimately arrived at the point of desperation and honesty. He cried out, "It no longer matters to me what I do or what I suffer, as long as I remain lovingly united to Your will."[*] With this confession, the floodgates of revelation and experience opened, and Brother Lawrence began to know Jesus in deeply profound ways.

Others eventually caught on to the special connection Brother Lawrence had with the Presence of God. However, it wasn't his exalted position that impressed people. His work was mundane to say the least—filled with hours in the kitchen and the humblest duties. He didn't experience success, at least not the kind that the world covets. Yet he seemed to constantly be under an open heaven, with blessings from God's Presence filling his life to overflowing.

Even in his day-to-day activities, onlookers were able to witness his spirit dwelling with his Heavenly Friend. Not only was he efficient and excellent in his work, but he also completed it with perfect peace.[†] By today's worldly standards, he wouldn't be considered notable. Thankfully, the true significance and impact of our lives are determined by God. We are simply called to know Him, love Him, and walk in friendship with Him all the days of our lives—now and for eternity.

---

[*] Brother Lawrence, quoted in Joseph de Beaufort, "The Life of Brother Lawrence," in *The Practice of the Presence of God* (New Kensington, Pa.: Whitaker House, 1982), 79.
[†] De Beaufort, "Life," in *Practice*, 82–83.

ACKNOWLEDGMENTS

The vision for this book was conceived twenty years ago when I was a seventeen-year-old praying at youth camp. I thank Jesus for walking with me in those twenty years—through my tears, fears, and failures—while never allowing me to shortcut the process.

To my husband, Dave: This book wouldn't exist without you. Your faith has strengthened me, and your love has championed me. Your friendship with God endlessly inspires me and challenges me. You have stood by me in my own wilderness seasons, and you have ushered me back to His Presence time and time again.

To my children, Moriah, Elias, River, and Adalynn: I have written this entire manuscript with you laughing and dancing around me. Being your mother is the greatest honor of my life, and it is the very reason I have learned how to practice the Presence of God. I love you more—always.

To my literary agent, Tom Dean, and the A Drop of Ink Literary team: In this journey together, you have been my cheerleaders every step of the way. You have been my answer to prayer, the means by which God made my twenty-year vision possible. Your seasoned insight and wisdom are priceless, but it's been your friendship and kindness that have made this so fun!

To my editor, Jamie Lapeyrolerie, and the WaterBrook team: Thank you for believing in this message with me. You and I both understood the God-given assignment, and we made quite the team. Your enthusiasm for this project has been an immense blessing to my heart. Thank you for challenging me to hone my voice and pushing me toward excellence. What a joy this process has been!

To Christine Caine: In my darkest days, you would ask, "Have you been preaching, Preacher?" You have taught me how to tenaciously hope against all hope while in my own wilderness. I will never forget it.

To our church, Mosaic Covenant Church of New Jersey: Life with you is like walking on water. Thank you for being my family's answer to prayer, our hope fulfilled, and our spiritual family. Let's continue discovering the worth of knowing Jesus together.

To the Honor Summit team: Your friendship and support through the wilderness have been a priceless gift to me. There are many more hills and mountains to climb, but I'll gladly climb them with you!

To Jesus Christ, my Lord and Savior: There is no better thing than knowing You. I love You with all my heart.

ABOUT THE AUTHOR

Faith Eury Cho has been a gospel preacher since she was nineteen years old. The mission of her life is for all to know and enjoy the gift of the gospel, which is the Presence of God. Alongside her husband, David Cho, she is the co-founder and pastor of Mosaic Covenant Church of New Jersey. With their four children—Moriah, Elias, River, and Adalynn—they hope to help people discover the worth of knowing Christ. Faith is also the CEO and founder of the Honor Summit, a nonprofit ministry that champions Asian American women in order to see all the church fully activated and equipped for God's kingdom work. She holds a master of divinity with a concentration in global studies from the Rawlings School of Divinity at Liberty University. *Outreach* magazine named her one of twenty rising leaders in 2023.